Theology with Photographs

Doing Theology with Photographs

Sarah Dunlop

LONDON • NEW YORK • OXFORD • NEW DELHI • SYDNEY

T&T CLARK
Bloomsbury Publishing Plc
50 Bedford Square, London, WC1B 3DP, UK
1385 Broadway, New York, NY 10018, USA
29 Earlsfort Terrace, Dublin 2, Ireland

BLOOMSBURY, T&T CLARK and the T&T Clark logo are trademarks of
Bloomsbury Publishing Plc

First published in Great Britain 2024

Cover image: *Contemplating the Change* by Sarah Dunlop, taken on a dusty road
in the foothills of the Sierra de las Nieves in southern Spain

A catalogue record for this book is available from the British Library.

Library of Congress Cataloging-in-Publication Data
Names: Dunlop, Sarah L. B., author.
Title: Doing theology with photographs / Sarah Dunlop.
Description: London ; New York : T&T Clark, 2024. | Includes bibliographical references.
Identifiers: LCCN 2023051116 (print) | LCCN 2023051117 (ebook) | ISBN 9780567713377 (pb) |
ISBN 9780567713407 (hb) | ISBN 9780567713384 (epub) | ISBN 9780567713414 (epdf)
Subjects: LCSH: Theology, Practical. | Photographs. | Communication–Religious aspects–Christianity.
Classification: LCC BV3 .D85 2024 (print) | LCC BV3 (ebook) | DDC 230–dc23/eng/20240213
LC record available at https://lccn.loc.gov/2023051116
LC ebook record available at https://lccn.loc.gov/2023051117

ISBN: HB: 978-0-5677-1340-7
          PB: 978-0-5677-1337-7
          ePDF: 978-0-5677-1341-4
          eBook: 978-0-5677-1338-4

Typeset by Integra Software Services Pvt. Ltd.
Printed and bound in Great Britain

To find out more about our authors and books visit www.bloomsbury.com
and sign up for our newsletters.

For Andrew, who often takes the photo I've seen, far better than I could.

Contents

Figures

Acknowledgements

I am forever grateful for Andrew Walker, who supervised my first piece of research with photographs. He took a risk on this unusual approach because he trusted me and believed in the project. None of this would have even got off the ground without his audacious support. May he rest in peace and rise in glory.

Pete Ward has been a long-term enthusiast for the work I have been doing with photographs – first with my PhD, then the post-doc and then subsequent publications. He told me years ago that I needed to write this book. Well, here it is, Pete! Thanks so much for believing in it, even before I did.

Over the years, several people have welcomed me on board their research voyages, only to find me adapting their projects by adding in work with photographs. Thank you, Andrew Todd, Andrew Davies, Mark Cartledge, Catherine Nancekievill and Pippa Ross-McCabe for giving me the freedom to experiment with your ideas. Working with all of you has been a huge privilege.

I've also learned so much from co-authoring pieces with some wonderful people. Philip Richter, who shares my love for photographs and theological research, let me take the lead on a book chapter. Catherine and Pippa – it was fantastic to write with both of you. And Jon Marlow, for taking the seeds I scattered and growing something beautiful. To all of you, my work is so much richer for having written with you.

For my precious friends, who cheer me on, especially when work + parenting + book seems like TOO MUCH. Thank you for your unwavering support and honest listening – Tanya Marlow, Ruth Perrin, Nellie Loh and Helen Alexander.

My colleagues at Ridley Hall, Cambridge, have been a phenomenal team of faithful and grace-filled peers. I love all of you.

So many people generously allowed me to use their photographs in this book. Thanks to Beth Bowers, my talented sister, for taking and sharing the photographs from Kyiv. Even during a house move you self-sacrificially found time to scan negatives. And much thanks to Ian Adams for not only sharing your stunning photographs, but also talking through your own spiritual journey with photographs. Your work and your generosity in sharing has opened new horizons for me. Thanks also to Ruth Barry, Sheryl Arthur, Pavlína Kašparová, and Mark Tatton – your photographs have added so much vibrancy to this book. Many thanks are due to my research participants for agreeing to take part and sharing your photos and your stories. I won't name you, as promised, but I am deeply grateful that you trusted me.

My parents, Dan and Paulette Bowers, have been a faithful team of supporters for all of my life. And finally, words cannot express how much gratitude is due to Andrew Dunlop, my friend, my love, my partner in life, for the firm belief in me. Laughing with you makes my life better. And Matthew and Anna – thanks for enduring all the photos – and for creating your own. I love doing life with you two.

1

Introduction: Affective Knowing

Figure 1.1 'Alone'. Photograph taken by a research participant as part of the 'Migration and Visual Culture: A Theological Exploration of Identity, Catholic Imagery and Popular Culture among Polish Young People' project, which was part of a Religion and Society Programme funded by the AHRC. Used with permission.

Seeing anew

A young woman produced the photograph above (Figure 1.1). The camera shows her perspective on a plate of half-eaten food, looking across the table at an untouched meal. She recounted that she had invited someone over for dinner and the person had not turned up, so she sat at the table alone. Again. She later discovered that there had been inadvertent confusion over time. Yet, in that lonely moment, she lifted her camera and captured this scene to portray what was sacred to her. Or, more specifically, to reveal a violation of the sacred. She explained in an interview:

> What is meaningful to me is community and being together and spending time together. I took this picture to show the lack of what is meaningful to me. When you eat alone, you just realise, God, how lonely I am! How loud the fork is when it touches the plate. I don't like it.

She explained that before she came to England from Poland, she had never eaten meals by herself. She submitted this photograph to an 'Images of the Sacred' project that I was leading with young Polish migrants to the UK. Her photograph portrays an everyday scene of the isolation of migration, and the spiritual need for social connection.

This is what this book is about. One does not need to be a professional photographer to do theology with photographs. I am not. Nor does one need to be a professional theologian. What is required is a curiosity about the gift that God might have for us as we pause, struggle, pray, think, notice, and form our theology.

Photographs and theology, although quite different in what they *are*, have similar traits in what they *do*. Both involve interpretation and personal engagement. As such, they work together in generative ways, functioning as key mechanisms for meaning making. I first came to use photographs to do theology when I discovered visual ethnographic methods during my PhD studies of the spirituality of young people in Ukraine.[1] Around this time, 2000–1, the Open University partnered with the International Visual Sociology Association to host a series of conferences in the UK called 'Visual Evidence'. I found that I was the only theologian amongst throngs of social scientists and documentary photographers. However, I met key contributors to the field such as Douglas Harper, John Collier Jr., Howie Becker, Marcus Banks, Sarah Pink, Elizabeth Edwards, and others.[2] By the end of the conferences, I became convinced that I should do more than study images in situ, I should use visual methods within the interviews.

---

[1] I tell more of this story in Sarah Dunlop. 2022. 'Visual Ethnography', in Pete Ward and Knut Tveitereid, ed. *The Wiley Blackwell Companion to Theology and Qualitative Research*. Oxford: Wiley-Blackwell, pp. 415–24.

[2] For more on the history of visual ethnographic research within the social sciences, see: Douglas Harper. 2000. 'The Image in Sociology: Histories and Issues', *Journal des anthropologues* 80–1: 143–60. https://doi.org/10.4000/jda.3182; Roman Williams. 2015. Chapter 1 in *Seeing Religion*. London: Routledge; Marcus Banks. 2018. *Using*

I needed to find a method that would help me look beneath outward cultural forms of religiosity in Ukrainian young people, and instead learn about what they believed in everyday life. I'd learned that visual methods took embodied cultural forms and practices into account. So, at the beginning of my fieldwork in Kyiv, I noted the posters, pictures and other images that formed the visual background of the lives of students. I took pictures and conducted interviews. Then, realizing that our conversation was limited by the content in the students' living space, I formed a collection of pictures, and interviewed the students about them. We flipped through the archive, and I asked the young people to choose which ones they would put on their walls. This worked well and gave me a breadth of responses to a variety of images. But still, I realized that I was controlling the interview content with my choice of pictures. And so, I then worked with a number of students, asking them to take photographs of what was significant to them and tell me stories about their pictures. My post-doctoral research used the same methods but expanded the context to young people in Russia, Hungary, Slovakia and Poland. This approach resulted in rich research data. I was able to see the students' life values and everyday spirituality in action through their photos and the stories they told. I came to see that just as Douglas Harper discovered that images enlarge the possibilities for doing sociology, so using photographs to do theology expanded the horizons of the theology that I could do.[3]

I called my first book *Visualising Hope*. By this I meant that I was looking for visible signs of hope within the student accommodation blocks that I visited. I also was referring to visual culture and how much we can learn, particularly about young people and youth cultures, by paying attention to their visual expressions. But what I mostly meant was the concept of visualizing. I wanted to learn more about young people's hopes, what they imagine their life could be or should be. John Wagner, a social scientist who theorized about visual research methods, argued that there are three concepts imbedded within the visual dimension: visible, visual, and visualize(d). Reflecting on the latter, 'the term "visualise" or "visualised" refers to neither objects, nor direct perceptions, but to a mode, process or dimension of understanding, a strategy of comprehension or conceptualisation.'[4] I like his definition, because it captures something of the meaning-making journey that I hope to learn more about as I conduct qualitative, visual ethnographic research.

Visual Data in Qualitative Research 2nd Edition. London: SAGE; Chapter 2 of Christopher Pole. 2004. *Seeing Is Believing: Approaches to Visual Research Vol: 7.* Leeds: Emerald; the Introduction in Sarah Pink. 2021. *Doing Visual Ethnography,* 4th edition. London: Sage; and Sarah Dunlop. 2022. 'Photo Elicitation' in S. Engler and M. Stausberg, eds. *The Routledge Handbook of Research Methods in the Study of Religion,* 2nd edition. London: Routledge, pp. 565–77.

[3]Douglas Harper. 1998. 'An Argument for Visual Sociology', in J. Prosser, ed. *Image-based Research.* London: Falmer Press, p. 38.

[4]John Wagner. 2006. 'Visible Materials, Visualised Theory and Images of Social Research', *Visual Studies* 21 (1): 55–69, p. 55.

How do we know about theology?

As an undergraduate at Wheaton College in Illinois, USA, I was required to take a Bible and Theology course. I was very keen to learn more about the Bible, because reading it had been a soul-nourishing experience for me during my teenage years. However, 'theology' sounded to me like thick, dusty books written by old men (mostly dead) in which they used invented words to describe complex philosophical concepts. I remember how I steeled myself to endure reading my first theological book – Augustine of Hippo's *Confessions*. I settled into a corner cubical in the university library, sighed, and opened the book. What seemed like moments later, a staff member approached me and said, 'What are you still doing here?' I looked around and realized that the library lights had been turned off. To my embarrassment, I'd become so engrossed in reading theology that I'd lost track of time and hours rather than minutes had passed by. At that moment I knew I'd discovered my new passion. I eventually changed my course so that I could spend the majority of my liberal arts degree focusing on theology.

I discovered that many of the core questions that I had wrestled with to make sense of the Christian faith had been topics of debate throughout history. I devoured the writings of ancient and modern theologians, hungry to take in more of the rich content. I remember catching my breath when I came across Anselm's 'faith seeking understanding' in his *Proslogion*. My soul resonated with his desire to discover more about God, which was not about helping him to believe. Instead, because he already believed, he longed to seek God's face. I loved how his writing was a heartfelt prayer:

> Speak now, my whole heart; speak now to God: I seek Your countenance; Your countenance, O Lord, do I seek. So come now, Lord my God, teach my heart where and how to seek You, where and how to find You.[5]

And so, theology, at its core, is faith seeking understanding. It is my conviction that theology entails the intellect, but it is also about sensing the presence and movement of the divine in everyday life. It is divine revelation to ordinary people like me. Eventually I came to see that theology was not just texts to *read* but was something that I could *do*. This book's title begins with '*Doing* Theology' because I want readers to see themselves as creators of theology and to pay attention to the theologies created by others. Theology is 'done' not only by scholars who write books, but the people we meet in everyday life. This perspective has challenged our epistemologies, creating the potential for scholarly theologians to be joined by people from all walks of life as 'knowers' when it comes to issues of faith.

---

[5]'Arousal of the Mind for Contemplating God'. *Proslogion*. 2000. *Complete Philosophical and Theological Treatises of Anselm of Canterbury*. Translated by Jasper Hopkins and Herbert Richardson. Minneapolis, MN: Arthur J. Banning Press, p. 90.

I now work within the area of Practical Theology, which John Swinton and Harriet Mowat have defined as 'think[ing] about practice theologically in a way that makes a difference to the ongoing life of the church'.[6] This interest in doing theology with faith practice in mind has led to a turn to empirical, usually qualitative, approaches to theological research, often with a focus on 'lived theologies'. This resonates with contemporary thinking around the importance of studies of 'everyday religion'.[7] Jeff Astley called for theology to take seriously what he called 'ordinary theology', described as the expressions of theological beliefs and processes of believing by Christians who have received little or no scholarly theological education.[8] Since then, we have seen that empirical studies reveal that people's expressions of their faith are a mixture of their spiritual experiences and the teaching they have received from their tradition.[9]

In the last few years, it has been argued that theology within a context exists in multiple layers or 'voices': formal, normative, espoused and operant.[10] Studying the formal, normative and espoused voices is relatively straightforward to study via interviews and literature searches. However, the operant voice, theology embedded within practice, is more difficult to pin down. Clare Watkins has observed that a core essence of the embodied nature of operant theologies is lost when reduced to verbal representations. She writes that this as an 'unresolvable paradox of articulating the "mute" ... voice of embodied theology'.[11]

This book addresses this concern by offering research with photographs as a means of studying the operant voice of theology. Many other scholars have noted that creative forms of research are uniquely valuable for drawing out stories of faith and embodied theologies. For example, Courtney Goto has explored how expressing a theological reflection via an art form enables a 'decentring' which can lead to 'an expanded notion of reflecting that gives form to the sayable and in ineffable'.[12] Clare Radford has described how 'creative arts-based' research methods are not only generative in terms of eliciting existing conceptions from participants, but the process of working with these creative expressions actually functions to generate theological knowledge that

---

[6]John Swinton and Harriet Mowatt. 2016. *Practical Theology and Qualitative Research*. London: SCM, p. 96.

[7]Within sociology of religion, this movement to empirical studies to learn about everyday religious practices was articulated by Meredith McGuire (see: 2008. *Lived Religion: Faith and Practice in Everyday Life*. Oxford: Oxford University Press) and Nancy Ammerman (see: 2007. *Everyday Religion: Observing Modern Religious Lives*. Oxford: Oxford University Press), amongst others.

[8]Jeff Astley. 2017. *Ordinary Theology: Looking, Listening and Learning in Theology*. London: Routledge.

[9]See our discussion about this in Pete Ward and Sarah Dunlop. 2011. 'Practical Theology and the Ordinary', *Practical Theology* 4 (3): 295–313.

[10]Helen Cameron, et al. 2010. *Talking about God in Practice*. London: SCM.

[11]Clare Watkins. 2020. *Disclosing Church: An Ecclesiology Learned from Conversations in Practice*. Abingdon: Routledge, p. 48.

[12]Courtney Goto. 2016. 'Reflecting Theologically by Creating Art: Giving Form to More than We Can Say', *Reflective Practice: Formation and Supervision in Ministry* 36: p. 80. http://journals.sfu.ca/rpfs/index.php/rpfs/article/view/426/413 [accessed 6 April 2020].

may have been previously unknown, even to participants themselves.[13] Zoë Bennett et al. observe that creative arts approaches enable engagement with homiletics, liturgy, sacred music and spiritual disciplines as 'creative practices' in and of themselves.[14] This book is my contribution to this conversation.

Photographs are a generative medium for doing theology because we 'know' with more than our minds, we know with our emotions and intuitions too. I call this 'affective knowing'. The importance of affective knowing for theology has been recognized by other scholars, particularly in terms of complexifying and diversifying our notions of what it means to be human. For example, Amos Yong has developed a theological anthropology that embraces disabled people. He outlines how, particularly within Protestantism, knowledge of God has usually been mediated through knowledge of doctrinal content.

> However, we have now insisted that this Platonic and Cartesian anthropology is faulty precisely because of its subordination of the body .... Insofar as the Hebrew *yada* refers more to the knowledge of the heart than the head, Protestants can now learn from Catholic and Orthodox traditions, especially with regard to how human knowing of God is mediated through formation, imitation, affectivity, intuition, imagination, interiorization, and symbolic engagement.[15]

James K. A. Smith charts an anthropology which emphasized that humans:

> are not primarily thinking things, or even believing things, but rather imaginative, desiring animals who are defined fundamentally by love. We are embodied, affective creatures who are shaped and primed by material practices or liturgies that aim our hearts to certain ends, which in turn draw us to them in a way that transforms our actions by inscribing in us habits or dispositions to act in certain ways.[16]

Smith is making the case for how worship functions within the lived experiences of people of faith. But what is interesting for doing theology with photographs is his view of people as 'affective creatures' with imaginations, not primarily thinking beings.

Photographs generate what pioneering visual sociologist Douglas Harper called 'a different kind of information'.[17] The brain processes visual images differently to words, meaning that when images are used in communication, they broaden the possibilities

[13]Clare Radford. 2020. 'Creative Arts-based Research Methods in Practical Theology: Constructing New Theologies of Practice', *Practical Theology* 13: 60–74. https://doi.org/10.1080/1756073X.2020.1727626 [accessed 6 April 2020].
[14]Zöe Bennett, Elaine Graham, Stephen Pattison, and Heather Walton. 2018. *Invitation to Research in Practical Theology*. Abingdon and New York: Routledge, pp. 152–4.
[15]Amos Yong. 2007. *Theology and Down Syndrome: Reimagining Disability in Late Modernity*. Waco: Baylor University Press, p. 208.
[16]James K. A. Smith. 2009. *Desiring the Kingdom: Worship, Worldview and Cultural Formation*. Grand Rapids: Baker, p. 137.
[17]Douglas Harper. 2002. 'Talking about Pictures: A Case for Photo Elicitation', *Visual Studies* 17 (1): 13–26, p. 13.

for knowing. This 'different kind of information' can be a form of theology that takes into account what we have called 'affective knowing'.

Rosalind Pearmain argued that because spirituality is held within the body, often experienced as a moving or stirring, investigating spiritual experiences using photographs is generative because the images connect to the bodily and affective forms of knowing. Drawing on the work of cognitive psychologists, linguists and philosophers, she argues that the body and mind should be seen as more closely connected. For her, meaning and imagination are situated not only in the mind, but also in the body. These 'presentational forms of knowing' allow people to access complex emotions, which operate alongside and in conjunction with cognition. This pre-conceptual knowing encompasses experiences, emotions and a person's sense of self. As Pearmain discovered, images can be put to work as evocative cues to draw out this affective form of knowing, leading to more profound discoveries. This creates a 'field of meaning' which is 'shared between researcher and participant as a relational and embodied experience, as something known because it is felt'.[18] This means that the possibilities for theology are expanded to include a wide range of mixed-ability people as theological knowers.

This book brings together the desire to know more about God and theology with the practice of photography. I will demonstrate how working with photographs will enable researchers and ministry practitioners to engage with their own or others' affective knowledge about God. Photographs can be used to illustrate and to document rituals and moments in time. Photography can also function as a performance of one's life.[19] Photographs elicit a range of emotional and psychological responses. They are a powerful medium for studying every day and operant forms of theology.

Doing theology with photographs

There are practical reasons for writing this book. Over the years I have had a succession of talented research students whose research I have supervised, many of whom have also discovered the value of using photographs within their projects. I am often asked to recommend a good book about using visual methods to study theology. There has not been one to direct them to, so, it has fallen to me to write it. Thus, this book flows out of a practical need and is practical in nature. The following chapters contain ideas, tips and examples to support the use of photographs within research and ministry practice. This book is not a philosophical treatise on aesthetics, nor do I propose a

---

[18]Rosalind Pearmain. 2007. 'Evocative Cues and Presence: Relational Consciousness within Qualitative Research', *International Journal of Children's Spirituality* 12 (1): 75–82, p. 80. Her observations are born out of a project in which she used an archive of photographs to explore spirituality with young people aged fifteen to eighteen.
[19]Gunilla Holm. 2008. 'Photography as a Performance', *Forum, Qualitative Social Research* 9 (2). https://doi.org/10.17169/fqs-9.2.394

doctrine of seeing. This book is not a technical guide for taking good photographs. There are plenty of other books, articles and websites that resource these important topics.

Instead, this book functions like a handbook. I assume that you, the reader, want to do theology and you are thinking about how photographs might support your endeavour. This book is for anyone doing research that explores theology, including spirituality, religion, values and rituals. This book will show you how to use photographs and visual material to generate rich data for your research project. It includes tips and examples from my own research and from other scholars working in their area. This book is also for people who are involved in Christian ministry leadership. I have seen that my students who have discovered the generative power of photographs within their studies have then taken adapted forms of these approaches with them into ministry practice. Thus, research with photographs has become ministry with photographs.

The first section of the book explores four methods of using photographs in research and includes details of the practical aspects of including visual material within a project. Chapter 2 describes a photo documentary approach, which entails taking photographs of a research context to record visual data. In Chapter 3, I describe how to elicit responses from research participants using an archive of photographs. In Chapter 4, I discuss how working with photographs provided by participants can yield useful data for a research project. Chapter 5 outlines a method I call 'narrated photography', a photovoice approach, which invites people to take their own photographs and then tell the interviewer the stories about their pictures. In Chapter 6, I offer a brief overview of how to analyse the visual material that is generated. I also explore some of the unique ethical challenges that accompany the use of photographs within research.

The second section of the book explores how photography may be used to resource ministry practices, theological reflection and spirituality. I demonstrate that photographs are a powerful means of opening new spaces for doing theology with people (Chapter 7), fuelling the theological imagination for reflection (Chapter 8) and supporting the spiritual practice of seeing and being seen by God (Chapter 9).

There is an element of the incarnational about doing theology with photographs because it entails engaging with the embodied nature of lived theology. Just as the incarnation of Christ was ultimately redemptive, so doing theology with photographs invites us to dispel the myth of objective observation and instead embrace the possibility of seeing divine transformation in action. My prayer is that those who take up the challenge of doing theology with photographs will discover so much more through this visual medium that they would never have learned by any other means.

Part I

Doing Theological Research with Photographs

2

Photo Documentary Approach: Telling the Story

Figure 2.1 Break-dancing on Khreschatyk in Kyiv. Photograph by Elisabeth Kay Bowers, taken for the 'Visualising Hope' project. Used with permission.

In my study of the faith lives of Ukrainian young people, I was interested in how young people were negotiating their place in the world when they were facing a context so immensely different from the older generations. This photograph of young men street dancing in front of McDonald's captures something of the global nature of youth culture in Kyiv at that time. Close inspection reveals that a street sign on the building (on the left side of the picture) says 'Khreschatyk', identifying this area as the central square of Kyiv, 'Maidan Nezalezhnosti' or 'Independence Square'. The boys are focused on the dance, and we see one poised to enter the cardboard square.

Their clothes and their activity do not distinguish them as Ukrainian, they could be in any country, dancing with their friends outside a fast-food restaurant. But they are distinguished from the crowd of people in the background, wearing big coats and fur hats, who look decidedly Eastern European. And so, this photograph tells something about the way young people are finding an identity within a landscape of post-Soviet monuments and corporate franchises.[1]

This is the first of the four chapters in this book which focus on visual methods for research. First, I'll explain what I mean by a photo documentary approach. I'll then share examples of people using this method to explore faith before sharing practical ideas about how this might work well in practice and what details may need consideration before using this method. The chapter closes with my perspectives on the advantages and shortcomings of this particular approach. The aim of each of these method chapters is to help you decide which visual methods you may wish to use in your own research. Indeed, you may find that a combination of methods would answer different aspects of your key research question.

Photographs as visual fieldnotes

Photography and anthropology both developed in the mid-nineteenth century and, since then, have at times overlapped and informed each other. Initially, photography was used as a research tool for cataloguing and recording a particular context. As such, the images assumed an objective, scientific stance towards their subjects, providing a qualitative, 'thick' description of the situation. This is evidenced in the work of early anthropologists like Bronislaw Malinowski, who used photography extensively in his research in New Guinea at the turn of the nineteenth century. Despite the challenges of using bulking cameras in the field, his written descriptions of the remote villages he studied are accompanied by hundreds of photographs. He reflected that a photograph captures an ephemeral moment of social life, similar to the way that an interview records a person's words in a given moment. However, he argues that the photographic representation should avoid making generalizing claims about the social situation.[2]

So, quite simply, what I am calling a 'photo documentary approach' entails taking photographs within the research context. These photographs are primarily used as a tool for documenting a situation for analysis. A qualitative research project may often involve a stage of participant observation and taking photographs in this

---

[1]This photograph was taken by a photographer, Elisabeth Bowers, whom I commissioned to supplement my own field photographs because I did not have a high-quality camera and I was not confident of my photography skills. I asked her to capture public scenes of youth culture.

[2]Michael Young. 1998. *Malinowski's Kiriwina: Fieldwork Photography 1915–1918*. London: University of Chicago Press, p. 19.

phase will help to capture useful information. On a surface level, these photographs function to record visual data for later analysis. The old adage that 'a picture is worth a thousand words' may indeed be true, especially when there is limited time to write fieldnotes. But, more than recording the visual landscape, the researcher can use the photographs to document and explain a context. This approach calls for paying careful attention to a situation and being curious about what is seen. It takes into account the visual aspects of a context that might otherwise go unremarked. I call this a photo documentary *approach* because the person using this method does not need to be a professional photographer or photojournalist. That's not to say that honing one's skills in taking good photographs is not recommended. But it is to argue that the purpose of taking the photographs is to document the context in conjunction with fieldnotes. Rose calls this 'photo-documentation', a method by which 'a researcher takes a carefully planned series of photographs to document and analyse a particular visual phenomenon'.[3]

Second, these photographs may also be used to present the findings of the research to others. Just as researchers may illustrate findings by writing verbal accounts of their fieldwork, so photographs can create visual narratives. A good photograph tells a story about what is happening in the frame.[4] As viewers interact with the image, they are interpreting what they see and creating meaning. This process can evoke emotional responses and open up new horizons for engagement with the subject. In this way the research data is interpreted again by another audience.

Walking with a camera

Liz Hingley, an award-winning documentary photographer who branched out into anthropology, conducted a photographic project 'Under Gods', a study of suburban faith in the Soho Road area of Birmingham, UK, in 2008–9.[5] She was interested in the growth of multi-faith communities, and the complexities arising from immigration, secularism and religious revival. She walked along the 2-mile stretch of road and photographed places of worship, and later, upon invitation, in people's homes. She photographed the spiritual practices of a variety of groups, including Sikhs, Buddhists, Hare Krishnas, Jamaican Rastafarians and The Jesus Army Christians. This project revealed the multi-faceted and adapting religious demography of the area.[6]

---

[3]Gillian Rose. 2016. *Visual Methodologies: An Introduction to Researching with Visual Materials*, 4th edition. London: Sage, p. 308.

[4]Or, the same subject could be photographed over time to show a progression. Another option is that a researcher may choose more than one image, perhaps a series of images, that recreate what the eye would see if the images were moving.

[5]Liz Hingley. 2010. *Under Gods*. Stockport: Dewi Lewis Publishing.

[6]Liz Hingley. 2011. 'Photographer/ Researcher: Notes from the Field of Faith', *Anthropology Matters* 13 (1). https://www.anthropologymatters.com/index.php/anth_matters/article/view/223/340

She was keenly aware of her own sensibilities, particularly as a British-born woman within this highly diverse context. She reflects, 'Increasingly I was conscious that my strategy for exploring the world embodied not just certain ideas but also beliefs about reality, gender, religion, the nature of subjectivity and the status of my subject matter in the wider public realm. There is no "ideal" position to which researchers can aspire; they have to maintain a reflexive, critical evaluation of circumstances and the ways in which these influence their work.'[7] She wrestled with her own positionality but acknowledged that, in the final analysis, her approach was based on a respect and fascination with the people she studied and the world in which they lived. Hingley's work is evidence that a photo documentary approach is valuable for research and yet, like any other qualitative method, requires a transparent reflexivity.

Camilo Jose Vergara, a photographer and sociologist, spent decades photographing churches in American slums.[8] Focusing on churches not in traditional buildings but instead in former storefronts, garages, factories, etc., he explored the worshiping lives of the poorest neighbourhoods of twenty-one different cities. His book includes more than 300 colour photographs which are accompanied with text from interviews with church leaders and congregation members. The book presents a portrait of how churches are signs of hope amidst impoverished and crime-ridden areas. What is striking about the book is how the visual material tells the story of the churches as points of hope in the darkness, with bright blue skies, sun shining on facades, creative use of ambient light to make the buildings glow. Although Vergara expressed an internal struggle as he experienced the various styles of Pentecostal worship, visually the story told is of these small churches as points of secret vitality within the drab streets of the slums.

Philip Richter has championed the use of photographs to explore Christian practice and the study of Christian congregations.[9] For example, he conducted a photography project whereby he walked the streets of three European cities on Sundays, taking photographs of his observations. Using these images, he created a photo essay that contrasted contemporary attitudes towards Sunday in three different locations.[10] He later argued in an article in the *Journal of Contemporary Religion* that photographs should be used in congregational studies because they can render the familiar unfamiliar through framing reality in surprising ways. This creates a critical distance from events and places, allowing researchers to revisit a snapshot in time and notice what may otherwise be overlooked.[11] He recommends that a study of

---

[7]Liz Hingley. 2011. 'Photographer as Researcher', *Visual Studies* 26 (3): 260–9.
[8]Camilo José Vergara. 2005. *How the Other Half Worships*. New Brunswick, NJ: Rutgers University Press.
[9]See 'Visual Methods' (with Sarah Dunlop) in Sylvia Collins-Mayo and Pink Dandelion, ed. *Religion and Youth*. Farnham, Surrey: Ashgate, 2010, pp. 209–16.
[10]Philip Richter. 2007. *Sunday: A Photo Essay*. Salisbury: Self-published.
[11]Philip Richter. 2011. 'Different Lenses for Studying Local Churches', *Journal of Contemporary Religion* 26 (2): 207–23, pp. 207–8.

a congregation could include a 'vicinity walk', in which the researcher 'allows the camera to take them for a walk', being curious about details and taking detours. He writes about discovering how 'photography is a slow release of meaning' which opens up possibilities for careful observations to develop into deep insights.[12]

Within my own early research, taking photographs during field research was admittedly initially ad hoc. I went into the field with my notebook, a small camera and a vague notion of what was I looking to shoot. I focused on snapping scenes that documented the visual environment of my context, particularly ads on billboards and in the metro. I was also interested in the use of religious icons and other objects as talismans. However, as my time in the field drew to a close, I reviewed my archive of photos and realized that, in a study about young people, I had almost entirely neglected to photograph any people at all! I was also disappointed by the low quality and haphazard framing of the images. I decided to work with an amateur photographer (who happened to also be my sister) to capture more of the kind of photographs I needed.[13] We spoke together about the kind of scene I was looking to illustrate, and she shot the pictures. Here is one example:

In Kyiv, wedding parties would go on tours of the city, stopping at monuments and other national symbols, such as folk performers, as pictured in Figure 2.2. I love the expression on the face of the man dressed as a Cossack. At a sacred moment such as a wedding, young people sought connection with their cultural heritage, which was no longer always accomplished by a service in the Orthodox church, due to residual antipathy against religion left over from the Soviet days. Another photograph showed a taxi driver with a series of icons inside the front of his vehicle. These photographs illustrate something of the transcendent within everyday Ukrainian life. Young people were seeking connection with their Ukrainian heritage on this significant day, and a *marshrutka*[14] driver was seeking divine protection with an icon at the front of his vehicle. As I reflected on these images, I realized that it was important to me not only to document the context and tell a story about what I found, but, as a theologian, I wanted to move beyond observing people's faith lives towards discerning and naming God's presence, action and people's hopes within a situation.

Several years later, when conducting case study research about chaplaincy for the Church of England, I took photographs to accompany my fieldnotes. Mostly these comprised photographs of empty prayer rooms or chaplaincy offices in hospitals,

---

[12]Philip Richter. 2012. 'Book Review: "Visual Research Methods in the Social Sciences: Awakening Visions"', *Journal of Contemporary Religion* 27 (1): 176–8. https://doi.org/10.1080/13537903.2012.643174

[13]In her study of the ecology of faith congregations on a street in Philadelphia, sociologist Katie Day worked with an urban photographer Edd Conboy. See Katie Day. 2014. *Faith on the Avenue: Religion on a City Street.* New York: Oxford University Press.

[14]Маршру́тка or 'route taxi', meaning a van that drives a set route. This is a common form of transportation in Ukrainian cities and is a cross between a taxi and a bus. Passengers pay a set price to the van driver, whose set route is designated by a number displayed in the windscreen.

Figure 2.2 Wedding party with musicians in Kyiv. Photograph by Elisabeth Kay Bowers. Taken for the 'Visualising Hope' project. Used with permission.

universities and other venues. We did not have ethical clearance for photographing people, so I was limited in what I could include within the frame. However, there were several occasions when a chaplain would share a symbol that encapsulated something significant, and, with permission, I took a photograph. This picture of a holding cross was taken in a hospital chaplaincy (Figure 2.3). The chaplain had just explained in an interview the importance of being with people in a very real, physical sense, as a way of offering spiritual support. He showed me the holding crosses that he would give to people, and demonstrated how it felt to grip the cross, and explained how this action became a form of prayer for people. This photograph of a material object came to encapsulate for me the vocation of chaplains to find creative ways to facilitate people's engagement with the divine in a variety of contexts.

In my own research, a majority of the photographs that I took were used merely as visual fieldnotes. Nevertheless, it is worth considering how to develop the skills of telling a theological story using photographs. The work of a social documentary photographer, Jim Grover, may serve as an example of producing photographs that say

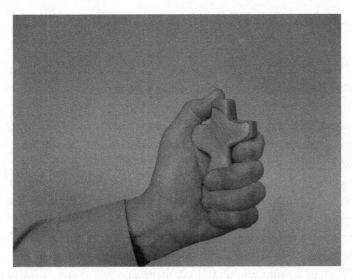

Figure 2.3 Chaplain's hand with holding cross. Photograph by Sarah Dunlop, taken for the 'Church of England's Involvement in Chaplaincy' project, commissioned by the Mission and Public Affairs Council of the Church of England.

something important about God's work in everyday life. Grover was commissioned by the Diocese of Southwark to create a photo-story as part of the celebration of the twenty-fifth anniversary of the ordination to the priesthood of women in the Church of England. Over a period of eight months in 2018–19, he documented the ministries of twelve women priests and conducted interviews with them. The photographs and accompanying texts formed an exhibit, 'Here am I', which was shown in 2019 in the OXO Gallery in London.[15] He captured these photographs by building rapport with female priests and asking them to ignore him as he just followed them and shot whatever they normally do. He also recorded interviews with his participants and asked questions such as 'Do you feel women bring anything distinctive to ministry? What lies at the core of your faith?'[16] It seems to me that the trust he built with these women, combined with listening to their stories, contributed to his ability to capture compelling photographs that portrayed the complexity and beauty of women's vocations. Grover reflected that when creating a photo-story, he aims 'to make seen the unseen'. Indeed, I would describe this as a process of doing visual theology, capturing something of the work of the transcendent God in the everyday lives of his subjects.[17]

---

[15]The photos and other information from the project are here: https://www.here-am-i.com. Jim Grover's other projects are 'Of Things Not Seen' www.ofthingsnotseen.com, a week in the life of a local vicar, and '48 Hours on Clapham High Street', portraying everyday life on a local high street www.48hoursonclaphamhighstreet.com. More about his can be found at http://www.jimgroverphotography.com

[16]https://www.here-am-i.com/an-interview-with-the-photographer

[17]His project 'Hope' is also an example of looking for something of God's hope within the everyday life of a community. http://www.jimgroverphotography.com/new-page-1

Documenting key scenes within the field

Although I stated above that one does not need to be a professional photographer to use a photo documentary approach method, certainly taking a class, joining a photography club, or reading some articles is helpful for learning to create more visually compelling images. Terence Heng has written a useful technical guide to creating strong photographs to use within qualitative, social scientific research.[18] Refining your photography skills may not seem important initially, as you seek to visually record a context, similar to pressing record on a voice recorder. However, later, when you want to tell a story about the situation, you'll find that the more engaging your images are, the better they will work to communicate with your audience through exhibitions, publications and academic papers. So, if you can, I recommend taking time to learn how to use your device well, whether it is a digital SLR or the camera on your phone. Indeed, make sure you are well practised in using your device because, when you are in the midst of your research context, you do not want to be uncertain about which setting to use or button to press. It is best to keep it simple and avoid using any settings which alter the image electronically while it is on your camera and shoot at the highest possible resolution. Any modifications to the photographs can be made later using software.

When taking photographs within a research context, it is a good idea to keep in mind the aim of the picture. Are you merely recording visual data for analysis later? This of course can yield huge volumes of information about what was happening at the time. If this is the case, then quick snaps may be all you need. However, if you are hoping that the photographs themselves will become forms of communicating your findings, then careful consideration of their formation is essential. Just as you would write up your findings in a clear and interesting way for a pithy and thought-provoking paper about your research, the visual material benefits from careful crafting in the same way. It may be that you take mostly un-staged, naturalistic pictures of the people and places that you observe. Or you may want to take posed photos in order to capture a particular event. In this case, it is often preferred to invite participants to choose how they are posed so that they can control how they will be represented.[19] Drawing on wisdom from photojournalism, Philip Richter suggested that considering how information such as what, why, when, how, where and who might be conveyed visually through the photograph is a helpful framework.[20] Of course, not all of these elements will always be shown in a single picture. It may be that

---

[18]Terence Heng. 2016. *Visual Methods in the Field: Photography for the Social Sciences*. Abingdon: Routledge.
[19]See Philip Richter. 2011. 'Different Lenses for Studying Local Churches', *Journal of Contemporary Religion* 26 (2): 207–23, p. 212.
[20]Philip Richter. 2017. *Spirituality in Photography: Taking Pictures with Deeper Vision*. London: Darton, Longman & Todd.

a series of photographs can be used and, of course, the caption can very helpfully give context. He argues that, overall, the photograph needs to attract attention and engage the viewer's curiosity. As a person gazes at the picture, they are invited to discover the narrative that lies within. The colours and lighting can be used to communicate the emotional texture of the scene. Avoiding a close cropping can help to give the viewer a sense of the context; at the same time, it is important to not crowd the image with too much clutter. Richter recommends asking oneself, 'If I could only take one photo of this, what would convey the story best?' And then narrow in on the subject, asking, 'What's the least I need to show to communicate what is happening here?' The idea is that the photograph should ideally draw in the viewers so that they want to spend time looking carefully at the image in order to discover what story is being told or to draw out a meaningful personal connection.

It's important to strategically plan what will be photographed in a setting. Starting with the physical surrounding of the situation, photographing landscapes and buildings, can help to set out the context. It may be less intrusive to photograph an empty church building, and this may be a good starting point. But is an image of an empty space the story you want to tell about this place? This may also be a good opportunity to begin meeting people in the community and explaining your research. This can lead to invitations to photograph and observe public events and maybe even family gatherings. It is important to take good fieldnotes to accompany your pictures, recording the day, time, people present, etc. You may want to also write your intention of creating the image, so that you do not lose a sense of why you took particular photographs and what struck you as significant at the time about the subject. These notes will be invaluable when you later create captions *with* rather than *about* the photographs that you use in publications or presentations.[21]

Photographing people is an excellent means of telling a story. Award-winning military photographer Jeremey Lock explained that he looks for two things in a photograph: a face and a story.[22] In Chapter 6, I'll explain more about the ethical considerations required for taking pictures of people.[23] For now, the main point here is that people often make compelling images and so you may want to photograph them. There are different ways of doing this respectfully and ethically. You can of course ask people for permission before you photograph them. If you need a more 'in the moment' type of photograph, you could take the photograph, and then show it to the person pictured and ask permission to keep the photo. If photographing at a church service or other event, you could ask the gatekeeper to notify the

---

[21]Philip Richter. 2011. 'Different Lenses for Studying Local Churches', *Journal of Contemporary Religion* 26 (2): 207–23, p. 208.

[22]https://www.picturecorrect.com/make-sure-your-photographs-tell-a-story/

[23]For a researcher's account of the issues encountered photographing people, including children, during Holy Communion church services, see Eleanor Nesbitt. 1993. 'Photographing Worship: Ethnographic Study of Children's Participation in Acts of Worship', *Visual Anthropology* 5 (3/4): 379–96.

people attending that photographs will be taken in a certain part of the space, so that people who do not want their picture taken can avoid that area. Jim Grover comments, 'I always find it interesting how quickly my subjects get used to me being around and, effectively, ignore me … which is exactly how I want it! If I am amongst groups of people then I will ensure that everyone knows who I am and what I am up to (also giving individuals the option of not appearing in a photograph, or telling me afterwards they don't want any photograph to be used with them in it). I always respect the privacy of individuals but have found that it's quite rare for someone to ask me not to include them in a photograph.'[24]

Liz Hingley planned the timings of her research of Soho Road around the best light in various locations, in order to make good use of optimal conditions for taking good pictures. The ability to use ambient light may feel less obtrusive within a setting than using a flash. However, this schedule also depended upon the timing of the services and events of the various faith groups. Additionally, she found it helpful to conceptualize photography for research as social engagement, not merely as an exercise in data collection. She invited the people she met to direct her gaze and to collaborate with her in framing the images and allowing people to express how they wished to be represented. She found that, as the project progressed, she took fewer photographs and spent more time listening to people. This helped her to understand the situation better, which then deepened her ability to capture the moment photographically.[25] She also found that moving quickly between contexts at times left her feeling disoriented and confused. It was important for her to take time between photo shoots to ground herself within her own familiar context and allow the vulnerability and ignorance of her experiences to fuel her creativity as she learned to see through other people's eyes.

Drawbacks and strengths of the photo documentary approach

One challenge of this approach is that taking a good photograph could get in the way of relating well to the people involved. Famously, Susan Sontag argued that photography may turn 'people into objects that can be symbolically possessed'.[26] However, as noted above, it is possible to have a real reciprocity between the photographer and the people being photographed. It's important to be engaging with the subjects of our research as living humans and picking up on subtle cues about their everyday lives.

---

[24]https://www.here-am-i.com/an-interview-with-the-photographer

[25]Liz Hingley. 2011. 'Photographer/ Researcher: Notes from the Field of Faith', *Anthropology Matters* 13 (1). https://www.anthropologymatters.com/index.php/anth_matters/article/view/223/340

[26]Susan Sontag. 1979. *On Photography*. Harmondsworth: Penguin, p. 14.

Concern for the technical side of a photograph, perhaps equipment set up or lighting, etc., could distract from the very real job of being present in the moment with the people involved. It's important to avoid becoming confined to the two dimensions of the photograph and acting as though we possess the people and objects within the frame. As Hingley noted, the subjects of the research can direct us towards what to photograph, advising on timings and explaining our presence. This then creates photographs that are collaborations between those behind and those in front of the camera.[27]

Another difficulty with this approach is that as the context of our photographs change, so can the way people interpret them. Particularly if people are viewing the photographs as works of art, the image may be considered to embody the perspective of the photographer-artist. We know that taking photographs of others inevitably portrays our own embodied experience. The camera captures the scene, but also the gaze of the researcher in that moment. But are others aware of this? Do viewers realize that the gaze may have been negotiated by the subjects? Alternatively, in the context of viewing a research report, people may read your research photographs as a 'true' record of the context rather than an art form. And so, people may believe they are viewing an unbiased visual report of events. Thus, careful consideration should be made of how to communicate one's own stance and perspective when using the images to tell the story of the situation. Dona Schwartz argues that attention needs to be paid to how viewers may substitute their own immediate reactions to photographs, drawing on their own experiences, rather than reacting to the photographer's intended meanings. She considers the pictures themselves to be inherently ambiguous, with their specific meanings emerging through the process of viewing and talking about the images. 'It is not the photographs themselves which inform, but rather, the analysis of them.'[28]

Indeed, an advantage of this approach is that analysing the photographs after the fact can lead to new insights into the social situation, opening up new lines of insight and enquiry. The research can pursue these new lines in further research, adding nuance and complexity to the study. Additionally, there may be elements of a situation that people do not speak about or acknowledge, perhaps because it is awkward or inconvenient. Or, people may be so used to doing things a certain way or become blind to certain aspects of their context, simply because they are overly familiar with them, and they have faded into the background. Recording with a photograph can help to literally bring these aspects of life back into focus, opening up new lines of conversation.[29]

---

[27]Philip Richter. 2011. 'Different Lenses for Studying Local Churches', *Journal of Contemporary Religion* 26 (2): 207–23, p. 215.

[28]Dona Schwartz. 1989. 'Visual Ethnography: Using Photography in Qualitative Research', *Qualitative Sociology* 12 (2): 119–54, p. 152.

[29]Liz Hingley. 2011. 'Photographer/ Researcher: Notes from the Field of Faith', *Anthropology Matters* 13 (1). https://www.anthropologymatters.com/index.php/anth_matters/article/view/223/340

Finally, a strength of the photo documentary approach is that, as Liz Hingley argues, a photograph invites the viewer to imagine themselves into the scene and wonder what lies beyond the frame. From her perspective, a photograph is not so much a realist recording of a moment in time, as it is a 'lyrical expression' that invites people to imagine the situation and discover something new about the real world that is inhabited.[30] It is a medium that invites people to question their reality, arouses curiosity, exposes them to a different view and to see through different eyes.[31] The photographer can shift angles of vision and open up new insights for doing theology.

Conclusion

The photo documentary approach to visual research creates data that are 'seeable', rather than merely 'sayable'. This means that the findings are shown, not merely written about in articles and books, or spoken about in lectures and papers. This leads to another level of knowing amongst the people who engage with our research. I've outlined some of the interpretative issues this creates, but it seems to me that this is worth navigating for the sake of the complexity of the layers of meaning available within photographs. Additionally, the visual format may be more accessible for a wider demographic of people, creating new streams of discourse about the research topic.

Two of the early pioneers of visual methods for research, Jon Prosser and Dona Schwartz, wrote,

> As image-based researchers, we have discovered the valuable contribution photographs can make, both in the practice and presentation of our work. Like our field notes and other forms of empirical data, photographs may not provide us with unbiased, objective documentation of the social and material world, but they can show characteristic attributes of people, objects, and events that are often elude even the most skilled wordsmiths … And we can provide a degree of tangible detail, a sense of being there and a way of knowing that may not readily translate into other symbolic modes of communication.[32]

Indeed, it seems to me that this 'sense of being there' is immensely valuable for developing a lived religion – seeing how people live out their faith in the everyday

---

[30]Liz Hingley. 2011. 'Photographer as Researcher', *Visual Studies* 26 (3): 260–9.

[31]Elizabeth Edwards. 1997. 'Beyond the Boundary: A Consideration of the Expressive in Photography and Anthropology' in M. Banks and H. Morphy, eds. *Rethinking Visual Anthropology*. London: Yale University Press, p. 53.

[32]Jon Prosser and Dona Schwartz, 'Photographs within the Sociological Research Process' in J. Prosser, ed. *Image-based Research*. London: Falmer Press, pp. 116, 131–47.

nature of their lives. Key to this is the 'way of knowing' available via photographs taken in the field that may not be translatable into written accounts. We will see in the following chapters how other approaches to using photographs can also resource these non-verbal ways of knowing.

3

Photo Elicitation from an Archive: Drawing Out the Story

We drew near the table. Ten people from different contexts stood encircling a library table laden with forty or so photographs of a variety of subjects. We'd been invited to choose a picture which spoke to our hopes. The facilitator's words 'What do you hope for?' resonated in my mind as I gazed at the many colourful images laid out before me. I had no preconception of what I would choose. In fact, I had not spent much time recently contemplating my life hopes, so I was curious what image might speak to me as I allowed my eyes to move from one to the other. Suddenly, a picture of a baby on the far corner of table, partly buried by others, caught my attention. I picked it up and my heart began to beat faster as I realized that indeed, the image truly encapsulated my deepest longings in that moment. The not-yet-realized desire to become a mother had lurked beneath the surface of my conscious mind. Yet it suddenly surfaced here.

In the previous chapter, I considered how taking photographs can be a highly generative aspect of a research project. In this chapter, we turn to how to use photographs and other material within the research conversation. We'll begin with an explanation about what 'photo elicitation' actually is. I'll then describe what this means in terms of working with an archive of images. Several examples of how this approach was developed will illustrate the features of this method. Then I'll give some practical advice about using photo elicitation within a project, before closing with a reflection on the strengths and weaknesses of this method.

Photo elicitation using an archive

One of the challenges of doing qualitative research is devising ways of drawing responses out of people that speak to our research interest. This 'eliciting' of information should of course be done with respect for participants. Those who are taking part in interviews and focus groups should feel able to not respond to a prompt that doesn't sit right with them. Ideally, the form of elicitation should also be engaging, igniting people's imagination and interest, so that they are eager to contribute. The last thing we want for a research conversation is for it to drag by and people to wonder when it will end. Therefore, researchers need to give careful consideration to their method of elicitation.

Most often, a carefully crafted set of questions are used to draw out responses from participants. They may be asked verbally, if the research conversation is taking place in person or via a call. The respondent them must consider what to say. This response is guided by the nature of the prompt. So, the words in the question frame the request for feedback. The person is then left to choose from a range of options, the most fitting response in this case. This thinking must then be translated back into words and articulated verbally to the interviewer or focus group facilitator. This process entails the participant interpreting the meaning of the words that the researcher has used and then formulating a verbal response. This highly cognitive activity can be used well to elicit useful data within a variety of interview scenarios.

However, what if the subject matter is a topic that people may never have spoken out loud about? It may be something that people have intuited, but never fully articulated. By asking for an initial verbal response, we are forcing them to translate into words something that they have only ever sensed. For this reason, I argue in this chapter that when researching issues around faith, spirituality and religion, visual prompts can elicit sensed reactions, resulting in data that include connotations as well as cognitive material. This process is called 'photo elicitation' when used as a research technique.

Philip Richter referred to this technique as a 'photo interview' because he was concerned that 'elicitation' may suggest drawing a response out of someone rather than inviting them to invest the image with their own personal meaning.[1] However, although this careful respect for the participant is admirable, I believe that referring to it as 'eliciting' information is precisely the aim of using the photographs – to draw personal reflections out of research participants. This by no means indicates that the responses are given unwillingly or that the photographs are being used as a form of manipulation. Instead, photo elicitation simply means that the images aid people to make connections which may enable them to talk about subjects that they may never have spoken of before.

There are multiple ways of employing photo elicitation methods, and we will explore three different approaches in this book. In this chapter, the use of an archive of images will be discussed. This entails the researcher gathering carefully chosen photographs or other visual materials and bringing these to each interview for use

---

[1]Philip Richter. 2011. 'Different Lenses for Studying Local Churches – a Critical Study of the Uses of Photographic Research Methods', *Journal of Contemporary Religion* 26: 207–23. http://dx.doi.org/10.1080/13537903.2011.57 3335

as prompts within the conversation. In Chapter 4, the method of using participant-provided pictures will be discussed. Then, in Chapter 5, we'll look at how to invite participants to create visual material specifically for use as prompts within the research project.

Examples: Evoking elements of human consciousness

The technique of using images to draw out comments and discussions in the course of a semi-structured interview or focus group was originally referred to as 'photo elicitation' in a paper by anthropologist John Collier in 1957.[2] In a study of the attitudes of people who had been resettled, he interviewed families twice – first, a 'control' interview using just conversation, then a second time using photos. He reported that,

> The characteristics of the two methods of interviewing can be simply stated. The material obtained with photographs was precise and at times even encyclopedic; the control interviews were less structured, rambling, and freer in association. Statements in the photo interviews were in direct response to the graphic probes and different in character as the content of the pictures differed, whereas the character of the control interviews seemed to be governed by the mood of the informants.[3]

Collier went on to champion the use of images within an interview. However, it did not develop into a mainstream research method within anthropology until twenty years later when John Wagner, building on Collier's work, included 'photographs as interview stimuli' in his list of visual sociology methods.[4]

Sociologist and photographer Douglas Harper was highly influential in extending and developing the method of photo elicitation within the sociology. More than prompts for accurate recall, he argued, 'Images allow us to make statements which cannot be made by words, and the world we see is saturated with sociological meaning. Thus it does not seem peculiar to suggest that images enlarge our consciousness and the possibilities for our sociology.'[5] Harper used his own photographs or archives of historical photographs of rural communities to explore how farming practices have changed over time. He found that using photographs gave participants a new

---

[2]John Collier, Jr. 1957. 'Photography in Anthropology: A Report on Two Experiments', *American Anthropologist* 59: 843–59.

[3]Ibid., 856.

[4]John Wagner. 1978. 'Perceiving a Planned Community' in J. Wagner, ed. *Images of Information*. Beverly Hills, CA: Sage, pp. 85–100.

[5]Douglas Harper. 1998. 'An Argument for Visual Sociology' in J. Prosser, ed. *Image-based Research*. London: Falmer Press, pp. 24–41 (p. 38).

awareness of aspects of their life they might otherwise take for granted.[6] Additionally, he observed that,

> … images evoke deeper elements of human consciousness than do words; exchanges based on words alone utilize less of the brain's capacity than do exchanges in which the brain is processing images as well as words. These may be some of the reasons the photo elicitation interview seems like not simply an interview process that elicits more information, but rather one that evokes a different kind of information.[7]

He also discovered that the images help to bridge cultural divides between the researcher and the participant. He observed that 'The photo becomes a bridge between people who may not even understand the extent to which they see the world differently.'[8]

Therefore, some social scientists like Harper and others have argued that the use of photos within an interview enlarges the possibilities for research. The visual functions like a mediator between what is unseen and sensed and creates what can be seen and spoken about. It is no wonder that I was attracted to this method as I embarked upon my own early forays into research as I wrestled with how to get beneath surface of nationalized, cultural forms of religion in order to study what in Central and Eastern European young people actually believed. In my travels in this region, I had noticed that religious images, such as Orthodox icons, hung on the walls of student accommodation alongside posters of Kurt Cobain or local figures from popular culture. I began to wonder whether, in a culture with a long history of visual imagery used in religious practice, placing an image from popular culture on a wall was a contemporary form of spirituality.

In former Soviet contexts, I was discovering that traditional religion was bound up with national identity. Yet, the remnants of Soviet atheism which sought to replace religion in society, combined with contemporary popular culture, formed a bricolage of meaning-making and spiritualities that operated beneath the surface of espoused traditional belief. Therefore, I designed my research so that images could do the work of drawing out some of these more subtle spiritualities. At the interview, instead of starting by asking my student-participants what they believed, I asked them to look through an archive of images that I had brought with me and to decide whether they would put them on their walls of their rooms in their student accommodation. The archive consisted of fifty images, developed through prior participant observation, and included pop culture images of sports stars, politicians, music artists, but also religious images such as traditional Orthodox icons, as well as images from other faiths and spiritualities. I also included prints of art and local landscapes. The aim

---

[6]Douglas Harper. 2001. *Changing Works: Visions of a Lost Agriculture*. Chicago: University of Chicago Press.
[7]Douglas Harper. 2002. 'Talking about Pictures: A Case for Photo Elicitation', *Visual Studies* 17 (1): 13–26, p. 13.
[8]Douglas Harper. 2012. *Visual Sociology*. London: Routledge, p. 157.

was to explore whether students used religious images in the traditional way, and additionally whether other images placed in their living space might tie in with expressions of identity.[9] This study revealed that the core values of young people, such as self-expression, freedom and fun were at odds with their perceptions of the values of Christianity.[10] Using photo elicitation with this archive enabled me to see their life values in action as they looked at the archive, chose the pictures for their walls and told their stories. I could not have come to these conclusions if I had just asked them about their spirituality or faith. From a sociological perspective, this method helped me to separate out the threads of a complex web of cultural influences. From a theological view, this approach meant that I could catch a glimpse of the 'lived religion' and everyday faith of the young people.[11]

Figure 3.1 Archive on a table, showing photos from *Every Picture Tells a Story: 48 Evocative Photographs for Inspiring Reaction and Reflection*, an archive created by Mark Oestreicher in 2013, used with permission. Photograph by Sarah Dunlop.

---

[9]Sarah Dunlop. 2008. *Visualising Hope: Exploring the Spirituality of Young People in Central and Eastern Europe*. Cambridge: YTC Press.

[10]Sarah Dunlop. 2008. 'Values and Significance: A Case Study Uncovering the Search for Meaning among Young People in Central and Eastern Europe', *Journal of Youth and Theology* 7 (1): 44–63. https://doi.org/10.1163/24055093-90000168

[11]See Nancy Ammerman. 2007. *Everyday Religion: Observing Modern Religious Lives*. Oxford: Oxford University Press and Nancy Ammerman and Roman Williams. 2012. 'Speaking of Methods: Eliciting Religious Narratives through Interviews, Photos, and Oral Diaries', in Luigi Berzano and Ole Riis, eds. *Annual Review of the Sociology of Religion: New Methods in Sociology of Religion*. Leiden: Brill, pp. 117–34. http://dx.doi.org/10.1163/9789047429470_007

Recently, I used photo elicitation again as part of a small research project, 'Exploring the reflective practice of Anglican laity: finding manna in the desert'. Working with two other researchers, we asked participants to share a significant life event, and then describe to us how they 'processed the event' or 'worked it through'.[12] We then asked them to choose a photo from an archive that encapsulated their 'processing' of the event. We also asked them about their processing of an event that happened in the last week, so that we weren't just gathering data about big life events. They also chose a photo for that more recent experience. We were pleased to observe that using photographs in this way opened spaces to talk about the intuited, imagined and felt nature of the process of relating life events to faith. This was important to us, because we were looking to see whether this processing was characterized by complexity, ambiguity and the provisional nature of knowing. The photographs enabled participants to delve deeper into the situation beyond a rational explanation and to access some of the emotional responses that they experienced. Additionally, images led some participants to make devotional statements of worship and to acknowledge the need to yield to God. Thus, again this method of photo elicitation with an archive gave me a glimpse of the intuited ways of 'doing' theology in everyday life. Additionally, as a theological educator, I discovered that I could use this approach within teaching to help students connect prior experience of reflection with more formal learning about theological reflection.

Thus, in these examples,[13] we see that photo elicitation with an archive can enable an interviewer to focus participants on a particular topic but also to widen the frame to include the capture of previously unspoken reactions. Images used in this way have the capacity to extend the potential of the research encounter beyond a cognitive response to set questions, because visual material operates on an intuitive and emotive level. This ability of visual stimuli to evoke elements of human consciousness is a powerful tool when used within a research project. But, particularly for practical theology, what is interesting is that this method may go beyond drawing out human intuitions and go farther by creating spaces for spiritual encounter. Sheryl Arthur used an archive of photographs within focus groups to study how members of a Pentecostal congregation live out their experience of 'Spirit baptism'. She invited participants to spend some time praying that the Holy Spirit would guide them to a

---

[12]Sarah Dunlop, Catherine Nancekievill, and Pippa Ross-McCabe. 2021. 'Exploring the Reflective Practice of Anglican Laity: Finding Manna in the Desert', *Journal of Practical Theology* 14 (4): 309–22. https://doi.org/10.1080/1756073X.2021.1957074

[13]For other examples, see Eleanor Nesbitt. 2000. 'Researching 8 to 13-Year-Olds' Perspectives on Their Experience of Religion', in Ann Lewis and Geoff Lindsay, eds. *Researching children's Perspectives*. Buckingham: Open University Press, pp. 135–49 and Sara Savage, Collins-Mayo Sylvia, and Bob Mayo. 2006. *Making Sense of Generation Y: The World View of 15-25 Year-Olds*. London: Church House Publishing. See also Linda Hopkins and Eleanor Wort. 2020. 'Photo Elicitation and Photovoice: How Visual Research Enables Empowerment, Articulation and Dis-Articulation', *Ecclesial Practices* 7: 163–86. https://doi.org/10.1163/22144471-bja10017

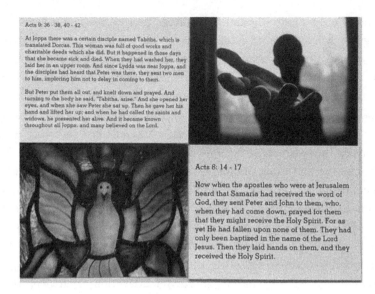

Figure 3.2 Spirit Baptism research. Montage by Sheryl Arthur. Used with permission. The images have a Creative Commons license and came from Pexels https://www.pexels.com/ and Pixabay https://pixabay.com/ [accessed 27 August 2020].

photograph that connected with their experience of Spirit Baptism (Figure 3.2).[14] She found that this method worked well, because within Pentecostal spirituality there is an expectation that God speaks through pictures. Additionally, she found that using an archive in this way opened up the possibility of discerning the mediation of the Holy Spirit through the interactions within the focus groups.

In the following section, I offer some practical considerations for putting this tool to use.

Using photo elicitation with an archive in a research project

Photo elicitation with an archive is, quite simply, bringing a group of images to a research encounter and using them to draw out a response from participants. The

[14]She had identified twenty-one Scripture passages relating to Spirit baptism and chose images from the internet that corresponded to each one. Each photo was printed onto a postcard and had the passage of Scripture printed on the back. Participants were invited to choose a photograph that related to their experience of Spirit baptism, and then share with the group about whether their experience related to the passage on the back. See the fronts and backs of two of the cards in Figure 3.2. Sheryl Arthur. 2022. 'An Elim Community Pneumatologically Engaged in Corporate Theological Reflection' in Helen Morris and Helen Cameron, eds. *Evangelicals Engaging in Practical Theology: Theology That Impacts Church and World*. London: Routledge, pp. 192–200.

archive is laid out or flipped through, and people are invited to pass comment, critique or reminisce as they gaze at the pictures. Photo elicitation usually employs photographs, but of course any other sort of visual image can be used, such as drawings, paintings, montages, graffiti, etc. Depending on the nature of the research project, images may portray events in a community, an urban landscape, historical scenes or a family snapshot.[15] With my research among young people in former Soviet countries, I knew that I would be asking them to choose which images they would put on their wall. So, I initially did participant observation, which gave me a chance to scope out what sort of images students tended to put on their walls. I then used this field data to form my own archive, which included appropriate poster-like images of pop stars, sports personalities, politicians, as well as aesthetic images including prints of fine art. Because I was interested in spirituality, I included overtly religious images. Years later, when I was conducting the study of how people make connections between everyday faith and life, I used a collection of photographs created to be ambiguous yet evoke a response from the viewer.[16] These worked well to help participants consider their processing of life events from an emotive, rather than cognitive angle. I have found that the choice of images must be closely tied to the area of the research question that the researcher needs to use the photographs to explore.

Related to this, when planning your own photograph elicitation, carefully choose questions that will guide the discussion about the photos. 'What does this remind you of?' is quite different from 'Which of these photographs do you associate with hope?' You could ask people to identify with the photographs, 'Which would you put on your wall? Which would you share on your Instagram?' Of course, some photographs generate discussion without much prompting, but it is always wise to be prepared with prompts just in case you need to help the conversation along.

Make sure that you choose photographs that people can relate to in some way. Random, unrelatable photos do not draw out interesting discussion, because time is wasted answering questions such as, 'What is this?' 'Where is this?' 'Why did you bring this picture?' It is worthwhile piloting the photographs on a select group to gauge reactions. Depending on your project, you may be able to use an already created archive of images. If so, experiment on yourself. I once asked participants to choose a photograph from an archive that represented their hopes. Before starting

---

[15]See Dona Schwartz. 1989. 'Visual Ethnography: Using Photography in Qualitative Research', *Qualitative Sociology* 12 (2): 119–54 for a detailed description of the process of taking photos and then using them in group interviews.

[16]A set of fifty numbered photographs produced by Soularium. https://www.cru.org/us/en/train-and-grow/share-the-gospel/outreach-strategies/soularium.html. On other occasions I've also used 'Gazing Prayer' cards produced by St Clare's at the Cathedral: https://stclaresatthecathedral.org/2018/05/16/gazing-prayers/ [both accessed 27 September 2022]. Another resource that I used for years was *Every Picture Tells a Story: 48 Evocative Photographs for Inspiring Reaction and Reflection*, an archive created by Mark Oestreicher in 2002 (updated in 2013) for use within youth ministry. Although these photographic cards were created with a specific Christian ministry in mind, I have found that, in the right context, they can work well for any kind of photo elicitation.

this research on other people, I tried it on myself, gazing at the pictures and asking myself the same question, to make sure that the photographs were suitable for eliciting helpful responses. You may instead need to create your own archive that is appropriate for your context and relates well to your research question. Historical photographs can also be used to draw out conversation about how the past may have shaped the present.[17] A related approach is called 'rephotography', whereby the researcher collects photographs taken in the past and then takes similar photographs at the current time. This approach can be used to draw out participants' reactions to changes over time.[18]

It is important to choose good-quality images that have some aesthetic value. People are more likely to talk about pictures that are pleasing to look at, even if the subject matter is not necessarily beautiful. Make sure all the images are the same good quality and roughly conform in size, material and shape. It is not helpful for your research if someone is thinking, 'I choose to talk about this one because it is printed on glossy paper and high quality. This one is not worth talking about because it is on cheap paper and the image is low resolution.' Number the images so that you can easily refer to them when creating a transcript of the interview. You can keep notes, or, if you are audio recording the interview, say something like, 'Ah, so you are surprised by this photo of the sea, number 18. Tell me why … ' You may feel silly at the time, but later, especially if you have more than one photo of the sea, you will be glad you specified. If you don't want to interrupt in this way, then you'll need to take notes. This is because when you are both looking at an image, much is assumed to not need to be said. For example, a participant might pick up a photo and say, 'I hate this one, it would give me nightmares.' And then put it down and move on, and you may forget which one was being referred to when you create the transcript.

Think carefully about how many you bring with you. If you bring too many, then the participant may spend a lot of valuable interview time looking through the photographs and not saying much. If you choose too few, and the participant does not find one he or she can relate to, then you will not elicit enough interesting conversation. I would suggest that an ideal amount might be somewhere between twenty and forty images, depending on your research aims and the length of your interviews or focus group. Furthermore, for the sake of consistency across a research project, it is advisable to use the same collection of images at every interview. This way you can test how people respond to the same images. In one of my projects, I wanted to understand how young people related to icons, so, at times I said, 'You

---

[17]Philip Richter describes how this could work in a study of a church congregation in Philip Richter. 2011. 'Different Lenses for Studying Local Churches – a Critical Study of the Uses of Photographic Research Methods', *Journal of Contemporary Religion* 26: 207–23, pp. 213–14. http://dx.doi.org/10.1080/13537903.2011.573335

[18]Bruce L. Berg. 2008. 'Visual Ethnography' in Lisa M. Given, ed. *The Sage Encyclopedia of Qualitative Research Methods*. Thousand Oaks: Sage, pp. 935–8.

flipped past this one, what do you think about it?' However, if there is an image that is causing problems, you could consider removing it, for the sake of the smooth running of your interviews. You would need to note this change in your methods section of your research report.

To summarize: the choice of images to include in the archive is absolutely crucial to the success of the study. Careful framing of the questions and talk surrounding the interaction with the archive is very important too.

Advantages and limitations of the method

The advantage of using an archive is that the researcher has a fair amount of control over the interview or focus group. The same photographs can be shown each time, enabling the researcher to compare different reactions and perspectives. By carefully choosing the subjects pictured within the archive, the researcher can guide the conversation along her chosen topic. Additionally, by bringing a prepared group of images, the researcher can ensure a consistency in the quality and format of the images. However, the apparent advantage of this level of control can also be this method's weakness.

One challenge is that finding the 'right' photos to draw out the desired conversation can be difficult. At times and in certain contexts, it may be nearly impossible to predict what sorts of images people will be able to relate to. Exercising control over choosing the images then limits the archive to the preconceptions of the researcher. Another limitation might be that the pictures have multiple interpretations, leaving people searching for the 'right' answer that the researcher requires. Vassenden and Andersson, in their photo elicitation study in Norway using photographs of religious buildings and books, discovered that because photographs may have a variety of meanings that could be discussed, it took young people longer to answer than it may have done if they were posed a more typical, solely oral qualitative interview question.[19] Nevertheless, they found that photo elicitation opened up their findings to avenues that they had not imagined beforehand.

Furthermore, a researcher may find that some people are more at home engaging with images than others. Communication in our world is increasingly visual. But we cannot assume that everyone is adept at reading images. For some people, being asked to use a photo to conceptualize something that may seem abstract, such as faith or hope, may be too far removed from their field of comfort. So, the approach

---

[19]Anders Vassenden and Mette Andersson. 2010. 'When an Image Becomes Sacred: Photo-elicitation with Images of Holy Books', *Visual Studies* 25: 149–61, p. 151.

may in fact exclude some people. In this case, the visual medium itself may restrict responses to the question. Thus, a project that uses other forms for elicitation, such as poetry, film, music or autobiography may yield rather different results and appeal to different people.

Nevertheless, I would argue that using an archive of images within a research conversation rather than relying on words alone is worth the risks because it opens up the possibilities for discussing emotions, vague memories, associations or connotations. For example, one colleague studied how rural church leaders were managing the large number of funerals during the Covid-19 pandemic and found that using an archive of photographs enabled Church of England vicars to talk about what they *hoped* a funeral service achieved for the family of the person who had died. Another colleague used an archive within interviews with ordained female preachers and found that talking through the archive opened up avenues for the women to speak about their emotional journey into the pulpit. Indeed, a simple explanation for the success of photo elicitation may simply be that as the interviewer and the interviewee gather around the images, less eye contact needs to be maintained since the attention is focused on the pictures. The conversation is slightly more relaxed because handling the pictures can fill gaps in the conversation.[20]

Conclusion

On one level, photo elicitation is a very simple research method. Photographs are used as part of an interview to spark conversation. Yet this chapter has aimed to demonstrate how including a visual element expands the possibilities for the research encounter. Most people experience life through multiple senses, and photo elicitation enables them to include what they see, their visual environment, within their response to our research questions. Douglas Harper, whose work to pioneer photo elicitation methods was briefly recounted above, argued that photo elicitation 'mines deeper shafts into a different part of human consciousness than do words-alone interviews'.[21] This means that photo elicitation increases the complexity of the data and theories that can be produced. For the practical theologian, this approach becomes a key method for exploring people's 'lived theology' as well as 'operant and espoused' theologies.[22]

Finally, we should not underestimate the importance of collaboration with our research participants. Harper also observed, 'When two or more people discuss the

[20]See John Collier and Malcolm Collier. 1986. *Visual Anthropology: Photography as a Research Method.* Albuquerque, NM: University of New Mexico Press, pp. 105–7.

[21]Douglas Harper. 2002. 'Talking about Pictures: A Case for Photo Elicitation', *Visual Studies* 17 (1): 13–26, p. 23.

[22]Helen Cameron, et al. 2010. *Talking about God in Practice.* London: SCM and Watkins; Clare. 2020. *Disclosing Church: An Ecclesiology Learned from Conversations in Practice.* Abingdon: Routledge.

meaning of photographs they try to figure out something together. This is, I believe, an ideal model for research.'[23] Indeed, the pictures not only provide a mechanism for building shared meaning, but this activity forms, in Harper's words, a 'bridge' between the researcher and participant. This is an exciting possibility for practical theology because these bridges between the researcher and research subjects create space for mutuality within the research encounter. Meaning is developed together as a person looks at photographs and relates them to their own story and God's story. Indeed, in Arthur's study, we saw that the archive was used to connect people to God via a process of waiting on the Holy Spirit. In this way, theology is done *with* people, not *for* people.

In the next chapter, we will explore how to increase the level of collaboration with research participants as we discuss using photo elicitation methods not with a researcher-provided archive, but instead with images possessed by the participant.

---

[23]Douglas Harper. 2002. 'Talking about Pictures: A Case for Photo Elicitation', *Visual Studies* 17 (1): 13–26, p. 23.

4

Photo Elicitation Using Participant-Provided Photos: Finding Photos

Figure 4.1 Pocket Holy Trinity. Photograph by Sarah Dunlop.

Olya* guides me through a bustling, open-air marketplace in Kyiv, packed with tables laden with a variety of wares. I pause at a stall selling icons and turn to my attentive host to remark that some of the icons are so tiny that it is difficult to distinguish which saint is depicted. She smiles at my lack of understanding and explains, 'They are for carrying with you. Look, I have one that I keep in my handbag.' She rifles around in her bag and pulls out a set of three small icons that fold together. She tells me, 'I call it the Holy Trinity. I always have it with me, for protection.' With her permission, I took the photograph above, in that moment (Figure 4.1). In this way, I discovered the fascinating potential of visual material already in the possession of participants. Without this exchange I may never have understood how these tiny sacred images function within the everyday religious lives of Ukrainian young people.

Building on the previous chapter, which introduced photo elicitation with an archive, in this chapter I explore another approach which uses the participants' own pictures to guide the conversation. The underlying principles of photo elicitation remain the same, but in this case, I focus on using personal images – those pictures that the participant possesses and volunteers to share with the researcher. Initially, I'll consider the role of the participant within the research. Then, I'll explore some examples of how this method has been used in practice. The next section offers ideas for how to use this method well. Finally, I'll describe the unique opportunities and challenges of including participants and their photos.

Participant-driven research

When photo elicitation methods were first trialled by Collier (1957) and later developed by Harper (2002), they both used an archive of images that they created for this purpose, as discussed in the previous chapter. This approach gave the researchers a strong measure of control over the content of the interviews. Just as within a formal interview, the interviewer brings the same set of carefully crafted questions, so in this case, using pre-proscribed sets of photographs brings a consistency to the conversations. However, over time, conceptions regarding the exchange of information within an interview have developed. Instead, we have come to see knowledge as negotiated and interviewees are 'participants'. Interviews are no longer limited to formal sessions of question and answer driven by the researcher, but instead, often are closer in nature to an investigator having a pre-arranged conversation with an informant. These semi-structured or informal interviews mean that the participant has more agency in the flow of the conversation.

Along similar lines, we could say that the style of photo elicitation in this chapter is 'participant-driven'. Instead of drawing a reaction from an interviewee using

---

*Not her real name.

an archive created by the researcher, here the participant plays a much larger role through providing their own photographs and other forms of visual material. The participants have the freedom to choose which images to speak about in response to the interviewer's prompt. They then guide the dialogue about the pictures, directing the initial interpretations of the visual material. As the interviewer and interviewee discuss the images, together they become co-constructors of meaning. This process of interpreting the image then opens a space for critically reflecting on lived experience. This approach expands the possibilities for the research interview. Both the stories that emerge and the visual material become rich sources of qualitative data.

Just as photo elicitation with an archive creates opportunities for participants to bring their affective associations to the photographs, so photo elicitation with personal images offers the same advantage. However, in this case, the images may hold long-established meanings and emotional responses. That is not to say that new readings will not emerge within the interview, but in this case, we are working with pictures that people are familiar with and may function as a backdrop to their everyday meanings. This means that the interview is an opportunity to draw out those meanings and invite people to tell the story that is associated with the image.

An advantage of using personal images over using an archive is that one bypasses the strangeness of the archive pictures. The participants will not need to spend time 'reading' the images as they gaze on them for the first time. Instead of puzzling over alien pictures, they are sharing photographs or images that already hold personal significance.

Essentially, by using personal images we are increasing the level of participation of the people that we interview. In this case, they are invited to offer more of their own selves into the research exchange. By providing a photograph from their wall, their albums or their phones, they allow the interviewer into their private space. This means that the visual data are entirely generated by the participants which increases the potential for their perspectives to shape research outcomes. This works well within a semi-structured interview approach, whereby the researcher comes to the interview with topics in mind to discuss but allows the interview to unfold more along the lines of a conversation, guided by the responses of the participant.

Examples of projects using found images

The use of personal pictures can help the researcher understand the relationship that people may have with images, shedding light not only on their uses in everyday life, but the meanings and associations attached to them. In this section, I include a series of examples in order the give the reader a sense of how this approach might work in practice. There are many ways that this type of research can be conducted. However, here I will focus on two key approaches: images displayed in the home and working with personal photo albums. It is useful to note that people may possess two different kinds of photographs. *Found* photos are those that they own and keep, and *taken* photographs were created by the participant.[1]

Two researchers influenced my own work in this area. In the UK, Paul Willis performed an ethnographic study of young people by studying their use of images in their rooms. He was fascinated by how teenagers used expressions, signs and symbols to creatively establish their identity and articulate personal meaning. 'Young people are all the time expressing or attempting to express something about their actual or potential cultural significance.'[2] Willis discovered that listening to them reading their own images revealed their inner imaginative life, their self-understanding and spirituality. In the United States, David Morgan investigated the role of mass-produced religious images and how they play a role in the social construction of reality by those who display them. He found that the meaning of an image is not merely the act of putting it on the wall, but also exists in its display and on-going presence in the owner's life. In this way, he argued that people use images to keep the chaotic universe at bay and to support and strengthen their existing world view.[3] The outcomes of these projects demonstrate that this method is useful for examining themes that are important for practical theology, especially spirituality, articulations of identity and constructions of meaning and significance.

Along these lines, I conducted a study of the images found in the rooms of students in Kyiv. As part of my study, I conducted participant observation, whereby I essentially spent time with students, observing and participating in aspects of student life. Through 'hanging out' in their personal spaces, I had informally gained a sense of what types of picture and posters I might find on student walls. When students agreed to invite me into their rooms for an interview, I asked them how long they had lived in the room, whether they were free to decorate the walls, and whether the images on their walls were placed there by them. But the key question of the interview was to discuss why they had put these particular images on their walls. As we talked, I discovered that students were aware of intentionally representing themselves through their images on their walls. I also asked students whether there were images that were important or significant to them that were not on their walls. At this point,

---

[1]Claudia Mitchell and Susan Allnutt. 2008. 'Photographs and/as Social Documentary', in J. Gary Knowles and Ardra Cole, eds. *Handbook of the Arts in Qualitative Research*. London: Sage, pp. 251–64.

[2]Paul Willis. 1990. *Common Culture: Symbolic Work at Play in the Everyday Cultures of the Young*. Milton Keynes: Open University Press, p. 1.

[3]David Morgan. 1998. *Visual Piety: A History and Theory of Popular Religious Images*. London: University of California Press. Later, in a book with Sally Promey, together they argued for the importance of including studies of visual material within our conceptions of religion within everyday society. They wrote that this kind of research should not be limited to high art, but instead should 'consider how all sorts of people live with all sorts of pictures in the public and private spaces of their lives' (David Morgan and Sally Promey. 2001. *The Visual Culture of American Religions*. London: University of California Press, p. xiii).

they might show me a photo album or one of their own drawings. I also asked them whether there was something they would like to put on their walls, but could not, for a variety of reasons (e.g. money constraints or negotiating space with a roommate). I discovered that the personal nature of the images and the resulting conversation opened up opportunities for the young people to share stories from their lives.

With permission, I took photographs of the walls as a way of collecting visual data, to work alongside my audio recordings of the interviews (Figure 4.2). I later used these photos as visual data for a content analysis. This entailed assigning a category to the different types of images I found, and then counting how many I found in each category, across all the interviews. I then analysed this data in terms of prevalence, which guided my approach to analysing the accompanying transcripts. This analysis revealed that placing an image of a famous person on the wall was a means of elevating their ideals, with a view towards communicating something about the students' own aspirations and negotiated identity. This piece of data was crucial for building up a picture of the emerging spirituality of Ukrainian young people.

Figure 4.2 Photos on a student's bedroom wall. Photograph by Sarah Dunlop.

A second approach to photo elicitation with participant's personal images is to invite people to reflect upon a theme using images from a photo album. A fair amount of research has been done on family albums, especially within the fields of art history and visual arts. Visual anthropologist Richard Chalfen, who pioneered research with 'home mode photography', argues that the album functions as a place to symbolically order the world.[4] Elizabeth Edwards stressed the importance of viewing personal photographs not only as material objects, but also as 'a form of interlocutors', since they function to unlock memories and produce new understandings of the self and one's cultural heritage.[5] Some scholars have researched their own family albums[6] and others have studied research participants' albums.[7] Many of these projects explore memory, identities and how self-understanding is reconfigured within the narration of the album. Art historian Mette Sandbye argues that family photos hold visual, emotional and social information and contain psychological and affective qualities that are important sources for humanities research.[8]

My own research has mostly engaged with digital albums or collections, rather than physical ones. For example, as part of a study of London Megachurches and their social engagement activities, I conducted a group photo elicitation interview with the members of one church located in the centre of London.[9] The participants had been asked to bring photos reflecting the theme of 'transformation' from their church-based social engagement activities. One woman provided the photo below (Figure 4.3) taken at a lunch club for elderly people living in the local area. I invited her to tell me what was happening in the picture, and she explained:

> After the meal there is some activity. This was about three months ago. It was a singalong in the programme of activities … One of the oldest guests in the room, a woman over ninety years of age, decided that she could not stay sitting, with this kind of music, she had to move along. So, she stood up and started dancing and invited

---

[4]Richard Chalfen. 1987. *Snapshot: Versions of Life*. Ohio: Bowling Green State Popular Press. See also: Richard Chalfen. 1991. *Turning Leaves: Exploring Identity in Japanese American Photograph Albums*. Albuquerque: University of New Mexico Press. Interestingly, he also studied images used in people's living space and in cemeteries in Japan and found that the practice of placing photographs offered information about the values and belief systems of that society. See: Richard Chalfen. 2003. 'Celebrating Life after Death: The Appearance of Snapshots in Japanese Pet Gravesites', *Visual Studies* 18 (2): 144–56, p. 144.

[5]Elizabeth Edwards. 2005. 'Photographs and the Sound of History', *Visual Anthropology* 21 (1–2 Spring/Fall): 27–46, p. 39.

[6]For example, see: Claudia Mitchell and Susan Allnutt. 2008. 'Photographs and/as Social Documentary', in J. Gary Knowles and Ardra Cole, eds. *Handbook of the Arts in Qualitative Research*. London: Sage, pp. 251–64.

[7]See, for example, Martha Langford. 2001. *Suspended Conversations: The Afterlife of Memory in Photographic Albums*. London: McGill-Queen's University Press, for a study that involves looking at other people's albums through a sociocultural lens. For her, photography is an act of communication.

[8]Mette Sandbye. 2014. 'Looking at the Family Photo Album: A Resumed Theoretical Discussion of Why and How', *Journal of Aesthetics and Culture* 6: 1–17. https://www.academia.edu/10122037/Looking_at_the_Family_Photo_Album_A_resumed_theoretical_discussion_of_why_and_how

[9]Mark Cartledge, Sarah Dunlop, Heather Buckingham and Sophie Bremner. 2019. *Megachurches and Social Engagement: Public Theology in Practice*. Leiden: Brill.

Figure 4.3 Dancing at ninety. From the 'Megachurches and Social Engagement in London' project. Photograph taken by a research participant and used with permission.

me to dance along. Initially I didn't really want to dance but eventually I stood up and joined her. This is the one who wanted to dance. (Pointing to the woman in a black jumper with a blue flowery skirt). She is over ninety!

Later in the interview, after discussing about ten photographs, I asked the group which was their favourite photo, and they chose this one of the impromptu dancing. I invited the participants to propose a title for the photo, and one person said:

> There is a quote from the Bible, isn't there about the time of abundance and plenty and it finishes with, 'and you will dance to the music of the tambourines.' I would call it that. I would find out where it was from (in the bible) and have that as well.[10]

We see that this group was using the photograph to start to connect an activity with scripture. Instead of using obvious passages about respecting elders or serving those in need, they are seeing how this ministry is creating a sense of generosity and security, which leads to an impromptu display of joy through dancing and singing. In the passage in Jeremiah, this dancing comes because of God's loving kindness and provision of security. I then asked the group whether they see God in this photograph. After a short pause, a person stated that what was happening in the photo was somehow an expression of God's joy, love and compassion. The person

---

[10]Most likely this is a reference to Jeremiah 31.3-4: 'The Lord has appeared of old to me, saying:
"Yes, I have loved you with an everlasting love; therefore with loving kindness I have drawn you. Again I will build you, and you shall be rebuilt, O virgin of Israel! You shall again be adorned with your tambourines, and shall go forth in the dances of those who rejoice."' (NKJV).

who offered the scripture reference observed that 'anything where somebody is reaching out to somebody else is an example of God's presence'. In this way, the group have developed a compelling theology of the active presence of God in the midst of these isolated elderly people. This photo captured a snapshot of a moment, intended to document a social engagement project's activity. But by using it within this group interview, it did so much more – stopping time and enabling the group to create an everyday theology of the moment.

Using participant-provided photos in research

In this section I will outline some ideas about how to use this method well. You will need to adapt these to your project, but the aim is to help you think through how using this approach will work in practice and what some of the some of the possible outcomes may be.

As discussed in the previous chapter, when using an archive for photo elicitation, the researcher exerts a large measure of control over the interview, delineating topics and responses. However, with personal images, the interviewer literally releases that control and must work with whatever the interviewee chooses to provide. This lack of ability to predict the course of the interview may be terrifying for the researcher, but there are certain techniques that can help to mitigate the unknown. First, when setting up the interview and discussing the information sheet, the investigator should let the person know that they will be discussing their own photographs and can check whether these are available. So, questions like, 'Would you be willing to show me your photo albums? What sorts of pictures do you keep in them?' will set the researcher's mind at ease before the meeting. Second, using participant observation, it may be possible to get a general sense of what kinds of images to expect. When I was studying the images on the walls of student accommodation rooms in Kyiv, I mentioned above that, before starting interviews, I had informal meetings with students in their rooms. I also kept a sharp eye on the kinds of photographs and posters that I saw on walls. This meant that I could formulate a list of categories of types of images that might be found on students' walls, and then devise appropriate questions in advance. Another approach is to combine photo elicitation with an archive in addition to personal images, meaning that just in case a participant did not have photographs that they could share, there was still plenty of meaningful conversation that could be had.

It is always the case that careful forward planning in advance of the interview will yield the best results, and this includes careful consideration of ethical research practice. In the case of using participant-provided photos, it is important that when the participant is invited to give informed consent to take part in the project, it needs to be absolutely clear that they will be invited to share some of their own photographs or images as part of the research project. If the researcher hopes to take photos of the images in situ, then this needs to be listed on the information sheet and consent form as a separate section, inviting the participant to grant permission specifically for this. The researcher should list how these images will be used – whether as a data source for the sole viewing of the researcher, or whether the images may be used later within another context, such as in a slide show during an academic paper or within a journal article or book. It is a good idea to check the copyright laws of your own government to see whether that the owner of the image giving permission is adequate or whether those pictured within should also grant their permission, if possible.

Additionally, when planning this type of research, it is important to consider the location of the interview. Ideally, the interview should take place in the participant's own space – their home, student accommodation or workplace. This is particularly important if, like my research, an aspect of the study is how images are used in living space. If photo albums are used, then it is helpful if the person has these books to hand. I specified in advance that the interview was intended to be with one person, because I found that student accommodation rooms were often public space, with people drifting in and out and roommates contributing their own thoughts. This was often quite fun (!) but made carefully planned ethical practice issues challenging. I also discovered that because of the personal location of the interview, bringing a hospitality gift was quite important, particularly in Central and Eastern European contexts. I was not only a researcher, I was a guest, which is a quite helpful dual role to keep in mind.

The interview itself is conducted quite similarly to any photo elicitation interview, as discussed in the previous chapter. The participant is invited to show their images and the interviewer gently invites responses along the theme of the research. In my experience, these interviews are often quite natural exchanges. When shown a photograph it is quite normal for anyone to show interest by asking, 'When was this taken?', 'Who are these people?', 'What is happening here?' or 'Why have you chosen this picture for your wall?' Once the participant has told a story or given the initial explanation, the interviewer can move on to dig a bit deeper, by asking 'If you were to give this picture a title, what would you call it?', 'What is the personal significance of this picture for you?'. Additionally, when planning interview questions, it is helpful to keep in mind what Banks distinguishes as two types of narrative that exist within a photograph: the internal narrative and the external narrative.[11] The internal narrative of a photograph answers the question 'What is this a picture of?' This yields descriptive information as well as interpretive. The external narrative is the story of

---

[11]Marcus Banks. 2018. *Using Visual Data in Qualitative Research*, 2nd edition. London: Sage.

how the photograph came to be created, answering questions such as 'Who took this picture? When was it taken? Why was it taken?' Thus, making sure to include both types of question will yield a wider range of data.

Challenges and limitations of the method

There are, of course, some challenges with using this method that should be acknowledged. A person may be willing to take part in the research, but may not have access to meaningful photographs, for a variety of reasons. Also, I discovered that the images placed on a person's walls might belong to someone else. Students in university accommodation said that at times posters and magazine clippings were left on the walls from the previous occupant, and they chose to leave them there. Another time I discovered that in one type of accommodation students weren't allowed to decorate their walls. I had to improvise with the less than ideal of route by asking what they would have liked to place there if they could! Another time, the images on the walls portrayed scantily clad women, and the participant said he felt uncomfortable discussing these images with me.

Many of these difficulties are due to designing this research to be driven by the participant, who provides the images. But the great value, of course, is that the images under discussion are already meaningful to the participant (unlike much archive research). In any kind of interview, the participant decides who they will be, what aspect of their identity they choose to share with the researcher. However, in the case of working with participant-provided images, I would argue that this choice may work differently. Of course, the person still has the freedom to choose what to share with the researcher and may indeed have placed specific images in the living space in preparation for the interview. Nevertheless, the interview cannot help but reveal some personal aspects of a person's life when working with their own images in their own living space. I think that this can lead to very rich conversations about a person's life and everyday lived theology. Of course, this open space for sharing personal details of one's life and faith needs to be carefully managed so that it does not become intrusive. However, I think this approach comes closer towards studying 'what is' rather than a reality a person wants to construct for the sake of the interview.

I have argued that the images become visual data, particularly if the researcher records them by taking photographs of them. However, careful consideration of needs to be taken of how this kind of data is analysed. When reading these images, it is of less concern, perhaps, to determine what is represented and what hidden meanings there may be. Instead, the primary concern is how the owner of the image interprets it.[12] So, if the owner is not the creator of the image, for the sake of this kind of research, the image needs to be narrated by the owner. Of course, the originator's intention may inform this reading, but it is entirely possible that it does not. Additionally, just as it is necessary to learn to 'read' text, so it is equally important to learn how to 'read' an image, particularly when working in different cultural contexts. Marcus Banks, when studying how people in India relate to religious images, discovered the Hindu practice of 'darshan' – 'seeing the divine' or the 'mutual exchange of looks'. In this cultural context, seeing is an active gaze, an interaction with the supernatural. Eye-to-eye contact between the images of the deity and worshiper formed an integral part of religious practice.[13] Thus 'seeing' is contextually bound, making it essential that the researcher collaborate with the participant to understand how their pictures function in their lives. Therefore, research images should not just be collected, but the owners or originators of the images should narrate their meanings and contexts.

Of course, this means that this method still relies heavily on verbal articulations of meaning. The participant is required to interpret the images that they bring to the conversation. This may privilege people who are more skilled verbally. However, it does open up a space for visual forms of communication, which many other text-based approaches will not.

Conclusion

It is important to remember that when we work with found photographs in this way, we are conscious not only of what a photograph *is*, but also what it *does*. Photographs can be interpreted as a means of recording events and documenting life, but their ongoing function in daily life may contribute to meaning making and coming to terms with life. For example, after my father died, I worked with my mother and siblings to collect photographs of him taken over the course of his life. We used these pictures to create a digital slideshow to be shown as part of his memorial service. After we had spent a few days organizing these photos, my mother remarked that this process had changed the nature of her grief. My father had died of dementia after a gradual decline took him from being articulate and energetic to frail and nearly comatose. She felt that the days spent with the photographs had caused her to shift from saying good-bye to the failing shell of my father to embracing the loss of the full person that he had been. Looking through the photographs and telling stories had reawakened her sense of him as a person, and helpfully complexified her grief. She was grateful for the important work that these pictures did in her.

---

[12]Theo van Leeuwen. 2001. 'Semiotics and Iconography', in Theo van Leeuwen and Carey Jewitt, eds. *Handbook of Visual Analysis*. London: Sage, p. 92.

[13]Marcus Banks. 2001. *Visual Methods in Social Research*. London: Sage, p. 8.

As discussed in the introduction, photographs and theology, although different forms and activities, function in simiar ways, because they both involve interpretation and personal engagement. Together they generate new meanings. Using personal photographs within a practical theology research project invites a deeply personal engagement with the research question. In the following chapter, we add another possibility to people's participation within the research, whereby the participant takes photographs as a response to the prompting of the researcher.

5

Narrated Photography: Centralizing the Vision of Participants

What on earth is happening here? I asked myself as I gazed at a photograph taken by a first-year Polish student (see Figure 5.1). We'd asked a group of students to spend a week photographing what was significant to them. The image showed a girl struggling to squeeze into an orange cartoon-character onesie that was clearly child-sized. The smile on her face and her impossible position made me laugh, imagining the giggles that must have been filling the room at the time. The interviewee explained this onesie was an excellent source of entertainment in her student accommodation: 'This is my sister dressed in a costume. It's gift that I got some time ago and during parties or when somebody comes to us it's always the best fun to make them wear it. It's so small that nobody fits into it, but there's always so much laughing with it and it's great fun.'[1] What astounded me was that this young woman chose this photo, out of the twenty that she took, to encapsulate what was most significant to her. Without this and other similar results from other participants, I may have never come to understand the importance of fun as a core value for young people. It also taught me about reading data with a willingness to be surprised and jarred outside my preconceptions. I'll explain later in the chapter how this initially perplexing image led me to discover some uncomfortable truths about students' unvoiced perceptions of religion.

The previous two chapters looked at how to use visual material within an interview or focus group as a means of eliciting a response from participants. That discussion is continued in this chapter, where we turn to considering using photographs that were generated by the participants for the purpose of the research project. To be honest, I love this chapter because I love this method. Having experimented with a variety of approaches, I truly believe that narrated photography is one of the best qualitative

---

[1]Sarah Dunlop. 2008. *Visualising Hope: Exploring the Spirituality of Young People in Central and Eastern Europe.* Cambridge: YTC Press, p. 41.

Figure 5.1 'Great Fun'. From the 'Visualising Hope' project. Photograph taken by a research participant and used with permission.

research methods for studying people's everyday faith. So, this is not a dispassionate description of another photo elicitation method, but unashamedly an argument for using this approach. First, I'll describe how I came to develop narrated photography. Then, I'll give examples of how I and others have used approaches like this. Next will be some practical guidelines for using this method in a research project. Finally, I'll explore some of the advantages and challenges of using this approach.

Narrated photography as a method for co-creating meaning

Narrated photography grew out of collaborative approaches to photo elicitation. A method called 'auto-photography' had already been used in social psychology, particularly in studies of the self. Participants were asked to take photos that portrayed a sense of 'who they are', with the aim of giving them a greater sense of agency within the research.[2] In a sociological study of a multicultural Dutch neighbourhood in 1997, research students collaborated with subjects on the production of the images, involving them in the framing of the photos and choosing which to be used in the interviews.[3] Wang and Burris went a step farther and invited their research participants to take photographs that were then used by the group to aid discussions evaluating the social situation.[4] They called this approach 'photovoice' and since then, other scholars from a variety of disciplines have employed a photovoice approach.

Photovoice is a method whereby participants are invited to take photographs by the researcher. 'Photo' because people are taking photos, 'voice' because of the perception that this method empowers participants to produce visual images that, as Guillemin and Drew argued, 'illuminate important aspects of lived experience that might otherwise have been overlooked or ignored by researchers'.[5] Thus, a visual 'voice' is given to people whose input may otherwise go unremarked. Putting the camera into the hands of the participants destabilizes traditional power imbalances between the researchers and participants. Informants literally frame what is significant to them according to their gaze.[6]

Photovoice produces valuable visual data. However, if the pictures produced by the method are used on their own, the images can be interpreted by the researcher or by others in many different and unintended ways. Although there is value in deeply engaging with 'reading' the visual data that is produced, it seems to me that my own interpretations are far less significant than those intended by the photographers. As I wrestled to develop a visual method, I knew I wanted to keep the empowering and collaborative elements of photovoice. But I also wanted the participants' input to carry on into later stages of the project, and so I incorporated the process of narration into the method.[7] It seems to me that the best way for research to empower participants is to invite them to become the storytellers of their own lives.

---

[2]See: Robert Ziller. 1990. *Photographing the Self: Methods for Observing Personal Orientations*. Newbury: Sage. Also Cassandra Phoenix and Noreen Orr. 2017. 'Engaging Crystallization to Understand Life and Narrative: The Case of Active Aging', in Brian Schiff, ed. *Life and Narrative: The Risks and Responsibilities of Storying Experience*. Oxford: Oxford University Press, pp. 235–50. https://doi.org/10.1093/acprof:oso/9780190256654.003.0013

[3]Patricia van der Does, et al. 1992. 'Reading Images: A Study of a Dutch Neighbourhood', *Visual Sociology* 7 (1): 4–68.

[4]Caroline C. Wang and Mary Ann Burris. 1997. 'Photovoice: Concept, Methodology, and Use for Participatory Needs Assessment', *Health Education and Behaviour* 24: 369–87. http://dx.doi.Org/10.1177/109019819702400309

[5]Marilys Guillemin and Sarah Drew. 2010. 'Questions of Process in Participant Generated Visual Methodologies', *Visual Studies* 25: 175–88. http://ddoi.org/10.1080/1472586X.201Q-502676

[6]See: Philip Richter. 2015. 'From Back Stage to Front: The Role of the Vestry in Managing Clergy Self-Presentation', in Roman R. Williams, ed. *Seeing Religion: Toward a Visual Sociology of Religion*. London: Routledge, pp. 103–21, p. 109.

[7]I give a more detailed analysis of this process in Sarah Dunlop and Peter Ward. 2014. 'Narrated Photography: Visual Representations of the Sacred among Young Polish Migrants in England', *Fieldwork in Religion* 9 (1): 30–52.

For social scientists, narrative is knowledge that sheds light on personal and public conceptions of a situation. Barthes and Duisit observed that narrative is a highly significant and universal form of communication. 'Like life itself, it is there, international, transhistorical, transcultural.'[8] Qualitative researchers have become increasingly interested in the power of storytelling as a mechanism for uncovering a social situation. 'Narrative research' was conceptualized by Denzin as an interpretive process that creates space for participants to be active agents who are invited to construct narratives to explain their world and their actions within it.[9] Chase outlined a concise history of 'narrative inquiry' within sociology, anthropology and studies of sociolinguistics and describes it as 'an amalgam of interdisciplinary analytic lenses, diverse disciplinary approaches, and both traditional and innovative methods – all revolving around an interest in biographical particulars as narrated by the one who lives them'.[10]

Within the field of practical theology, Swinton and Mowat argue that when planning a research project, it is often not enough to merely observe the behaviour of people, but instead it is necessary to give them the opportunity to narrate their lives, thus allowing them to interpret their actions in the context of their own view of reality.[11] Then, the audience of the narrative become co-creators of the emerging meanings, engaging in the tensions presented by this narrative, 'messy approach', in Denzin's terms.[12] For Chase, not only the audience, but particularly the researcher becomes a 'co-creator of the narrative' with participants within the interview, who then reflexively continues this interpretive process in analysis and reporting. This approach to co-creating meaning through drawing out narratives from participants fit well within my conceptions of how I hoped the participant-generated photographs would work within the interview.

So, narrated photography combines a narrative enquiry approach with photovoice and uses this within photo elicitation.[13] Collecting the stories linked to the photographs is absolutely essential. Although photographs capture a moment in time, similar to a memory, they do not preserve meaning. As Bach argues, photographs 'offer appearances, a sign – with all the credibility and gravity we normally lend to appearances – prised away from their meaning. Meaning is the result of understanding

---

[8]Roland Barthes and Lionel Duisit. 1975. 'An Introduction to the Structural Analysis of Narrative', *New Literary History* 6 (2): 237–72, p. 237.

[9]Norman K. Denzin. 1997. *Interpretive Ethnography: Ethnographic Practices for the 21st Century*. Thousand Oaks, CA: Sage, p. 246. http://dx.doi.org/10.4135/9781452243672

[10]Susan E. Chase. 2005. 'Narrative Inquiry: Multiple Lenses, Approaches, Voices' in Norman Denzin and Yvonna Lincoln, eds. *The SAGE Handbook of Qualitative Research 3rd Edition*. London: Sage, pp. 651–80, p. 651.

[11]John Swinton and Harriet Mowat. 2016. *Practical Theology and Qualitative Research, 2nd Edition*. London: SCM Press.

[12]Ibid., p. 247.

[13]Sarah Dunlop and Peter Ward. 2014. 'Narrated Photography: Visual Representations of the Sacred among Young Polish Migrants in England', *Fieldwork in Religion* 9 (1): 30–52.

functions. Functioning takes place in time, and must be explained in time. Only that which narrates can make us understand. Photographs in themselves do not narrate.'[14] Therefore, the photographs hold people's experiences and meanings which are then used to elicit the stories of the experiences and their meanings.

As Guillemin and Drew argue, this type of method 'takes seriously the participants as knowers'.[15] Jointly with the interviewer, participants are invited to become co-creators of the emerging knowledge. Indeed, by its very nature, narrated photography is collaborative – not only in inviting the participant to provide the images but also inviting them to invest them with their own personal meanings and interpretations.[16] Additionally, the participant is empowered to choose their own level of engagement with the research question. The process of composing photographs gives people time to choose how personally or superficially to picture their response. This is helpful in terms of considering research ethics, because participants retain control over how much personal information they are willing to share and are given ample time to consider this.

The value of this approach is that it mirrors the way that people may already be making meaning within everyday life. Flory and Miller, in their research of the spirituality of young people, observed that people in contemporary society are not only immersed in images and digital media, but that they are also producers of this visual environment. 'Rather than being passive observers of the products of these digital tools, people are now active participants in producing, reproducing, and manipulating images, conversations such as on blogs, music and the like.'[17] Moreover, not only is this a participative approach, but the method itself is a highly accessible activity, because most people, regardless of education or language skills, can take photographs and speak about them on some level.

Finally, narrated photography is more than a method, it is also a product of the research. The images and accompanying text together embody the abstract concepts of the participant and when exhibited together, the text and pictures narrate the lived

[14]Hedy Bach. 2001. 'The Place of the Photograph in Visual Narrative Research', *Afterimage* 29 (3): 7. https://online.ucpress.edu/afterimage/article-abstract/29/3/7/191563/The-Place-of-the-Photograph-in-Visual-Narrative?redirectedFrom=fulltext
[15]Marilys Guillemin and Sarah Drew. 2010. 'Questions of Process in Participant Generated Visual Methodologies', *Visual Studies* 25: 175–88, p. 177.
[16]There is a tradition of visual research being developed for the sake of including and empowering participants. See, for example, the argument of Douglas Harper. 1998. 'An Argument for Visual Sociology', in J. Prosser, ed. *Image-based Research*. London: Falmer Press, pp. 24–41. Also, the ground-breaking work of Sol Worth and John Adair. 1972. *Through Navajo Eyes: Explorations in Film Communication and Anthropology*. Bloomington: Indiana University Press. Also Cindy D. Clark. 1999. 'The Autodriven Interview: A Photographic Viewfinder into Children's Experience', *Visual Studies* 14: 39–50 and Jo Aldridge. 2012. 'The Participation of Vulnerable Children in Photographic Research', *Visual Studies* 27: 48–58. http://dx.doi.org/10.1080/1472586X.2012.642957
[17] Richard Flory and Donald E. Miller. 2007. 'The Embodied Spirituality of the Post-Boomer Generations', in Kieran Flanagan and Peter Jupp, eds. *A Sociology of Spirituality*. Aldershot: Ashgate, pp. 201–18, p. 201. See also their 2008 book, *Finding Faith: The Spiritual Quest of the Post-Boomer Generation*. Piscataway, NJ: Rutgers.

experience of the participant. Thus, the challenge for the researcher is to combine textual and visual mediums when reporting the findings. Reports of the interview data should include the pictures, and, in the same way, an exhibition of the images should be accompanied by excerpts of text drawn from the photo elicitation interviews. In my own research, I have found that a public exhibition of the photographs, accompanied by short quotes from the transcripts, functions as an accessible means of communicating the research findings back to a community. Those who attend the exhibition can be invited to respond, thus adding another layer of interpretation and analysis that emerges from the context itself.[18]

Experimenting with narrated photography

I alluded to an example of narrated photography from my own research in the opening vignette of this chapter. As the principal investigator on a project, 'Visualising Hope', which took place in five locations in Central and Eastern Europe, I worked with local researchers to study the spirituality and religious attitudes of students in these regions. The research took various forms and included interviews with church leaders and well as photo elicitation interviews with young people, using an archive of images. Additionally, five students were chosen in each city to take part in what we called the 'photography project'. We asked them to spend a week taking three pictures a day for a week, of things that were significant to them (objects, places, people and moments of significance). 'Significance' was defined as 'that which tells us who we are and gives a sense of purpose to our existence'. The researchers had a preliminary meeting with each student to explain the project and give him or her a page of written guidelines. At the follow-up interview, the students narrated their photographs, and then they were asked to put them in order of importance. We invited them to give a title to their five most significant photos and tell us why they made the top of the list.

Through the lens of their cameras the young people showed us a glimpse of student life. The students seemed to enjoy making the photos. Many of them playfully staged pictures to show that having a little bit of fun is important to them. An example of this, in addition to the story at the start of this chapter, came from an interview with a female student in Nizhny Novgorod, Russia. She summed up the significance of a photo of an ad featuring a large yellow smiley face: 'This is fun, laughing, entertainment. Naturally, it is important for me. One can't live without it at any age, especially at my age, in student's life. I mean not just studies but also having fun.'

---

[18]For a summary of my exhibitions on Religion and Polish Migrants, see this BBC report: http://news.bbc.co.uk/local/devon/hi/people_and_places/religion_and_ethics/newsid_8370000/8370409.stm

Additionally, a Polish student had a photo taken of herself and a friend playing on the city's public transport as though it was a playground. 'These are small crazy things that add charm to the life. That's me with my friend in a tram that I ride home every day.' Another student, this one in Kyiv, took a photo of himself and his roommate wearing sunglasses and sitting in the toilet block of the student accommodation. He liked to play with creating staged images, showing the real parts of his life but at the same time having fun with it.

As I analysed this visual and textual data, I realized that when the young people ranked what was significant to them in order of importance, they had shared with me their values. And it was fascinating that, after relationships, having fun was one of their highest values. This may not seem hugely earth-shattering. Students like to have fun, so what? However, the data revealed a clash between students' values and their perceived values of the Christian church. The interviews revealed that young people thought religion as not fun, which meant that it was ruled out as an option for how to spend their limited free time. The use of visual material was key to this finding, because for many young people, living in societies where faith was bound up in national identity, they were unlikely to initially state that Christianity was not fun.[19]

I used the narrated photography approach again when I conducted a study of the religious beliefs and practices of young Polish migrants, aged eighteen to thirty in Plymouth, England.[20] Since 2004, large numbers of young Polish people have settled in Great Britain, and I was interested to discover what happens to the faith of these young people after they move from a country with a traditional, Roman Catholic religion to the UK which is a substantially more diverse and pluralist religious context.[21] Through connections made via participant observation in Polish businesses and Roman Catholic churches in Plymouth, I invited potential participants to a photography workshop which included an explanation of the research project. Participants were invited to spend a week taking ten photographs representing what is sacred to them. I chose to focus on what was 'sacred' (rather than religious) in order to draw out both formal and informal religious practices. A few weeks later I interviewed the participants, using their photographs to guide the conversation. The questions were informal, 'Would you tell me what is happening here?' Or 'Who are these people?' Or 'Why does this represent what is sacred to you?' Then, the participants were asked to choose which photograph best expressed what

---

[19]Sarah Dunlop. 2008. *Visualising Hope: Exploring the Spirituality of Young People in Central and Eastern Europe.* Cambridge: YTC Press.

[20]This section draws on material in my chapter 'Photo Elicitation', in 2022, M. Stausberg and S. Engler, eds. *The Routledge Handbook of Research Methods in the Study of Religion*, 2nd edition. London: Routledge, pp. 565–77.

[21]The results of this study are recounted in Sarah Dunlop and Peter Ward. 2012. 'From Obligation to Consumption in Two and a Half Hours: A Visual Exploration of the Sacred with Young Polish Migrants', *Journal of Contemporary Religion* 27 (3): 433–51. https://doi.org/10.1080/13537903.2012.722037.

was 'sacred' to them and to compose a title for it. These photographs, the titles and quotes from the interviews were then used to create an exhibition held in the local Roman Catholic Cathedral. The young people came together again at the launch of the exhibition and, as a group, responded and interacted with the photos and the themes they raised.

An unexpected finding was that the images that emerged from the project portrayed a particularly Polish Catholic lens for seeing the landscape of Plymouth. For example, a young woman photographed a statue of Mary set into a wall near the Barbican, a bustling district of Plymouth full of shops, cafes and bars. It is a battered statue salvaged from a lost cargo of marble from a ship which sank off the coast of Plymouth. A plaque below it reads, 'Stella Maris', which refers to Mary as the Star of the Sea and Patron Saint of all mariners. The young migrant explained that this encapsulated the sacred to her because …

> We are attacked from every side by adverts and the media. They seem colourful, but they are only temporary, because they won't last for long, they will put up a new advert. But this statue seems to be more permanent. Not only because it is the symbol of the Virgin Mary, but because it looks so stable, if you compare it to other things which are around it and changing constantly. This is so stable. And the Virgin Mary is meaningful to me, she emanates peace and calm and says to me, 'Don't worry'.

Figure 5.2 'The Solid Structure of Life'. From the 'Migration and Visual Culture: A Theological Exploration of Identity, Catholic Imagery and Popular Culture among Polish Young People' project, which was part of a Religion and Society Programme funded by the AHRC. Photograph taken by a research participant and used with permission.

She called her photo 'The Solid Structure of Life'. For her, this photograph embodied the sacred because Mary symbolized divine protection. Living in a time of personal instability and uncertain about the future, she was drawn to the stability of this statue.

So, we see that inviting the participants to photograph, rather than just talk about, the sacred necessitated an engagement with their visual landscape, which revealed how their everyday religion affects how they inhabit public space. In this case, statues and buildings in the city of Plymouth that may have faded into the backdrop of the urban landscape for residents were literally focused upon by the Polish young people, rendering a whole new, religiously charged view of the city. Using narrated photography brought the physical element of space together with the social and spiritual, providing a rich means for studying the participants' everyday, lived religious beliefs and practices. We literally 'see' the spiritual longing of young migrants in a strange new city.

Others have also made interesting discoveries when using methods similar to a narrated photography approach. For example, Hopkins and Wort were pleased to observe first-hand how photo elicitation and photo voice, when used together, empowered their participants, changing them from passive objects of study into 'emancipated co-creators' of research.[22] They also noted the co-creative potential of visual methods for doing theology. They found that visual material enabled more than an articulation of faith, it opened up the possibilities for 'dis-articulation', meaning that participants were able to use images when words were not adequate.

Gemma Foster developed what she calls a 'Digital Image Journal' to study what is helping emerging adults grow in their discipleship. As an experienced ministry leader among people in their twenties and thirties, she is aware that technology and social media permeate all facets of their lives. She wanted her research method to mirror the ways that this demographic already communicates in everyday life. So, she invited participants to use their smartphones to take a photograph each day for a month that described their relationship with God or Jesus and post it on a private Instagram feed. They were encouraged to post a title or other text to accompany their photo and also to like or comment on other participant's posts. In the interview at the end of the month, they were asked to choose a few photos that reflected something of their faith journey over the past month. She discovered that using the 'journal' concept meant that participants were encouraged to upload a photograph every day, which helped to gain insight into the ordinary ways that people conceive of their relationship with God.[23] Doing this project as a group added a layer of accountability, because the group got to know each other through the posts, which created a form of online community. Foster found that using images meant that the project included people who may not have felt confident communicating verbally about their faith. She

---

[22]Linda Hopkins and Eleanor Wort. 2020. 'Photo Elicitation and Photovoice: How Visual Research Enables Empowerment, Articulation, and Dis-Articulation', *Ecclesial Practices* 7: 163–86.
[23]If they had nothing to 'say' on a day, they could upload a blank screen, as a way of continuing the daily habit of the journal, but removing pressure to produce an image every day.

noted that the digital image diary method worked well, because 'participants were keen to share about their images, the stories and experiences which were happening that were encapsulated through the image. They offered a window to another world which photography had captured in time – a fleeting moment which may have likely been forgotten, but through photography was a documented spiritual experience. During the interview process the images came alive to me as a researcher as the participants spoke about what was happening in their images.'[24]

Planning a project using a narrated photography approach

Several aspects of a narrated photography project are worth considering carefully before starting empirical research. First, the question or prompt that you will set for your participant to guide them as they take their photographs is essential to get right. Simply asking them to take photos related to your main research question may not, in fact, elicit a helpful response. To test a prompt, I would suggest setting yourself the challenge. Think of a question, then spend a week or so taking photographs yourself along that theme. You could ask a couple of friends to do it too. Buy them a coffee at the end, look at their photos and talk about what was good about the question and what might not have worked so well. Refine the question. I found it helpful to define what I mean by key terms. If I was working among people from a different culture to my own, I would check with native speakers about how the key words translate and whether other words might be better.

Second, plan your timescales carefully. This method works best when you hold an initial meeting with participants to talk through the photography project and give an in-person, warm invitation to take part. This means that you can clarify any questions that people may have about the key theme or technical questions about the mechanism of taking, saving, and sharing the photos. I have found that holding a photography workshop with participants at this initial meeting can be very fruitful. A professional photographer could offer basic techniques to help participants take better quality photos. The hands-on activity of taking photos enables participants to begin to think about the creative power of visual communication, and to ask informal clarification questions about the project. Additionally, I like the idea of giving something of value back to participants who are investing parts of themselves in my project.

Given the potentially open-ended nature of narrated photography, it is advisable to limit the amount of time given to participants to take photos. This will hopefully help them to give focused attention to their photography project. They need to have

---

[24]Gemma Foster. 2023. 'Methodology' of PhD Thesis, University of Manchester, Cliff College.

enough time to give the task some thought and planning, but not so much time that they forget to do it. In light of this, it is also advisable to limit the number of photos that you ask participants to provide for the interview. With digital photography it is possible to take literally thousands of images. The time within the interview is much more productively used if participants have pre-selected five to fifteen images that they would like to talk about within the interview. So, the timescale needs to take into account the initial meeting, the time to take the photographs, and then the final interview. I would advise holding the final interview quite close to the conclusion of the period set for taking the photos, so that the intentions behind the images do not get lost as time passes. Related to this, at the initial meeting, participants could be asked to keep a journal, video diary or some other means of recording their thoughts as they take their photos. This gives participants time to consider how they will frame their thoughts and how much of their personal, private life they will share during the interview.

Third, as always, the interview itself needs to be carefully planned. Since the photographs are central to the conversation, their format needs to be considered. The participant could email them or place them in an online shared folder. They could bring them on a USB drive or some other means. In this case, it will be important to have a device with a good screen for viewing the images. Alternatively, at times I have asked to have the pictures in advance of the interview, and made two sets of prints, one for myself and for the interviewee to keep. The advantage is that they can be laid out so that all of them can be viewed at once. Whatever the format, it is important to be able to distinguish which photograph the participant is talking about during the interview, for the sake of the audio recording. I often find it simplest to just number the photographs and make handwritten notes. Or I can refer to them using the number within the interview, so that in the transcript I see questions like, 'So, you are saying that this photograph, number 4, is the most significant for you? Why is that?'

Fourth, the interview questions still need to be prepared, even though the images are, in a sense, the main interrogators. Quite simple prompts can work quite well:

- Why did you take this photograph?
- What were you feeling when you took this photograph?
- Which of these photographs best expresses the theme?
- If you were to give this photo a title, what would it be?

In most cases, the participant and the photographs drive the conversation, rather than a series of questions. Simply saying, 'Wow – these pictures look great. Talk me through them' can be enough to get the participant started, because the theme set by the researcher has already guided the creation of the photographs. If the pictures are printed and laid out, then the interviewee can decide which image to start with. If using a digital collection, then it is possible to use a similar approach by showing a screen of thumbnails. Additionally, some researchers have found that it is helpful to follow a particular sequence of questions within the interview, in order to ensure that they are drawing out comments that move from observations towards analysing the visual data. Wang developed these questions, which she calls SHOWeD:

S – What do you **S**ee?
H – What is really **H**appening here?
O – How does this relate to **O**ur lives?
W – **W**hy does this situation, concern or strength **e**xist?
D – What can we **D**o about it?[25]

This approach is particularly helpful when used within a Participatory Action Research project, or something similar, whereby an aim of the research is to move towards some form of responsive action.[26]

Figure 5.3 *Sacred Images*, an exhibition at Greenbelt of photos from the 'Migration and Visual Culture: A Theological Exploration of Identity, Catholic Imagery and Popular Culture among Polish Young People' project, which was part of a Religion and Society Programme funded by the AHRC. Photograph taken by Sarah Dunlop.

[25]Caroline C. Wang. 1999. 'Photovoice: A Participatory Action Research Strategy Applied to Women's Health', *Journal of Women's Health* 8 (2): 185–92, p. 188.
[26]See how Roman Williams adapted these questions for his research within a church in his article: 2019. 'Engaging and Researching Congregations Visually: Photovoice in a Mid-Sized Church', *Ecclesial Practices* 6: 5–27. https://doi.org/10.1163/22144471-00601002.

Finally, as mentioned above, 'narrated photography' refers to both the method and the output of the research. Therefore, planning some form of exhibition as part of the research project can be highly generative. The photographs should be accompanied by the narration from the participants. One way to do this is to put up a card alongside each photograph that includes the title given to it by the photographer, and an excerpt from the interview that speaks to the theme of the project. Or participants could simply be asked to write their own narration to accompany their photo. An exhibition serves multiple purposes. It can be used to generate additional analysis from participants, who may be invited to view and comment upon the pictures. Or the general public may also be invited to respond to the exhibition via a comment book or social media. The exhibition can also be a means of reporting back some of the findings to a more varied audience than those who would read an academic report.

Of course, there are times when we may want to share the visual evidence within a presentation via a screen. I think that this is a really important aspect of communicating the findings of research. Not only is it visually engaging, but it draws the audience into the worlds that participants inhabited. Initially I created slides with the image and the quote from the interview beside it. However, I found that people tended to immediately read the text and then glance at the photo, whilst I may have continued speaking. I sensed that my approach was sidelining the visual data. So, I have started to click onto the new slide which contains only the image. Then, after waiting a few moments, I then click again to bring up the accompanying words. This then gives the visual material more of a focus within the presentation and allows viewers time to engage visually.

Limitations and advantages of the method

On balance, in my opinion the advantages of this method outweigh the drawbacks. However, there are some challenges that require careful consideration. For example, using this narrated photography approach takes time. Over the years, I have come to expect that any empirical research that I do will wind up taking twice the time that I imagine it will. Using this method requires multiple meetings, time allocated for participants to take the photos, and then the follow up interview or focus group. This is not an insurmountable problem, and careful planning can make this work.

A second limitation might be whether the medium itself restricts responses to the question. Not everyone is adept at translating a theoretical theme or question into a visual form. In the example of the young Polish migrants above, participants were asked to photograph what was sacred to them. This produced a lot of photographs of nature – does this point towards the sacralization of the outdoors? Or is it just easy to take a good photograph of a landscape? When testing the photography exercise on oneself or others, the researcher needs to be prepared to face that the question itself may not lend itself to a visual expression. Either the theme or the wording of the question needs to be shifted, or, in fact, a new method needs to be employed. Also, there may be situations in which photography is not possible. Rachelle Green's study of theological education in a prison invited participants to make drawing of 'the good life' as a means of eliciting responses within a focus group, because any kind of photography was prohibited within the prison.[27] Additionally, a colleague who uses photographs to help people explore their vocation spoke about how a blind participant remarked that using an object in place of a photograph worked well in her case. In sum, when planning a project using narrated photography, it will be important to consider whether this method might need to be adapted according to the context or participants.

Finally, a drawback of using narrated photography is that the researcher has relinquished control of the visual data into the hands of participants. This means that it is difficult to ensure the quality of the photographs produced. I have received photographs that are sadly out of focus or blurred. People have sometimes had a lot of very useful things to say on the key topic of my research, but the accompanying photograph is less than ideal, due to the framing or composition. I think this is a risk that we just have to embrace when we put the camera into the hands of others. If you are working with an institution that is imagining a professional photography exhibition to result from your project, you may have to manage their expectations. Furthermore, ethical considerations around the use of these images will need to be carefully managed. The following chapter will provide some important guidelines for considering ethical research practices when working with visual material. But it is worth noting here that relinquishing control of the production of images may mean that some of the photographs will not be able to be used in the reporting of the project because participants have not sought the required permissions.

Much has already been written above about the advantages of a narrated photography approach. It seems to me that it comes down two key advantages: the medium and the nature of the method. First, the medium of the still image is a unique form of data. It captures a snapshot of a moment and by stopping time, enables the full range of meanings to be explored via the interview and analysis. Because the photographer-participants have produced a narrative that invests their images with personal meaning, the resulting collection of images and text mediates the subjective into a form that is perceptible, thus making the intuited concrete and open for study. This process highlights the individual's personal signifying themes, which

---

[27]Rachelle Green. 2022. 'Ethnography as Critical Pedagogy: Prisons, Pedagogy, and Theological Education', in Pete Ward and Knut Tveitereid, eds. *The Wiley Blackwell Companion to Theology and Qualitative Research*. Oxford: Wiley Blackwell, pp. 38–48.

enables a study of the complex ways that faith is woven into everyday life. Using photography in this way takes into account the visual landscape that is inhabited by the research participant.

The collaborative nature of narrative photography is an advantage that should not be underestimated. Banks and Zeitlyn observed that giving informants cameras avoids 'swooping god-like into other people's lives and gathering data (including visual "data") according to a pre-determined theoretical agenda [which] strikes us not simply as morally dubious but intellectually flawed'.[28] Indeed, the participants are empowered and at greater ease, because they are already fully familiar with the photographs, and not trying to work out the meaning or significance of researcher-provided images. This approach has been proven to provide rich and interesting data.[29] Not least because in advance of the interview, participants have reflected upon the subject of the project through taking photographs. This means that the interviews or focus groups are conversations that are often more well-considered than the 'off the cuff' responses that other approaches might otherwise elicit.

Conclusion

I love narrated photography as a method for doing theology. It brings me back to my vocation as a practical theologian. I've always wanted to do theology that matters to people in their everyday lives. People's own lived theologies are embodied in practice and physical spaces. Narrated photography expands the possibilities of our theology because we can literally see how people view their faith in everyday life. It also increases our ability to be highly self-aware as theologians, increasing our awareness of our own preconceptions, power and position. I think that narrated photography is a natural development in research methods for practical theology, given that the camera on a smartphone, combined with social media apps, means that people are regularly documenting visual personal meanings. Finally, the photos themselves, as exhibited or otherwise disseminated, do not only tell the story the researcher is telling, but they *show* the story. We are actually seeing a vision of reality, not just reading about it, or listening to it. This showing is a powerful means of communicating one's world.

---

[28]Marcus Banks and David Zeitlyn. 2015. *Visual Methods in Social Research*. London: Sage, p. 165.
[29]Patriciavan der Does, et al. 1992. 'Reading Images: A study of a Dutch neighbourhood', *Visual Sociology* 7 (1): 4–68.

6

Analysis and Ethics: Planning Research with Visual Material

In the previous four chapters, I laid out the key methods for using photography within qualitative research. Now the question moves from 'How does one use photographs for researching everyday theology?' to 'Shall I use one or more of these methods in my own project?' The key to answering this question is to carefully consider your research question. What aspects of your question do you need the empirical research to answer? In my early research, I tended to use a mixture of methods. This was because I was still learning to trust what each method achieves. I also was hedging my bets – if one method failed, I would have the others to fall back on.

So, once you've identified which aspects of your research question you aim to address with a specific method, it is important to do a good bit of background reading about the method. Read multiple case studies from other researchers who have used similar approaches, paying close attention to the advantages and challenges that they encountered. Document all of this reading carefully, because it will most likely form a section within your methodology and methods sections of your research report or dissertation. Particularly if your supervisor is new to visual research methods, your critical analysis of the literature will be key for their support.[1] You can also include some of this material in a research proposal for your department or research grant application. I've included a lot of the key sources in this book, but your own searches will yield the most recent and applicable literature for your own project. There are two other issues that require your attention as you plan a project using visual methods: ethical practice and data analysis.

---

[1] Indeed, when I first pitched my ideas for using photographs to my PhD supervisor, he expressed concern that taking pictures would not constitute actual fieldwork. I managed to convince him by writing a thorough review of scholarly literature regarding visual methods. Later, when I wanted to make a case for including photographs within the text of my thesis, again I drew upon publications about visual material as evidence within field reports.

Ethics of using visual material

One of the most delicate aspects of planning research using photographs is navigating ethical clearance. In many senses, applying for ethical clearance for a project using visual material is nearly the same as it is for any qualitative research project. Assuming that you are already familiar with your own institution's policies and procedures regarding ethical practices and data privacy, this chapter will raise a few issues that are specific to research with visual materials, particularly relating to privacy laws, consent and confidentiality.

When using a photo documentary approach, it is important to research the laws that apply to photography in public spaces in your research context. In the UK and the United States, anyone may take photographs in public places.[2] Legally, one does not need to ask for permission to take a photograph of a person or their children in a public place. One can also take photographs in privately owned places which are open to the public, such as shopping malls and restaurants, unless the owners ask people not to. People are entitled to a reasonable expectation of privacy, so the more public a place is, the less expectation a person is entitled to. However, there are public places where someone may still have a high expectation of privacy, such as the public toilets in a park. The International Visual Sociology Association code of ethics states, 'Visual researchers, like other members of the public, have the means and right to record images that may, at the time, not seem invasive. Subsequent use of these images must be circumspect, given legal standards of public domain and fair use standards.'[3] There may also be rules within an institution or organization that the researcher will be expected to adhere to. It is also important to remember that the storage of research images will need to follow data protection regulations.[4]

Thus, the starting point is to make sure what you are proposing in your ethical clearance application follows the existing laws and rules. The next step is to carefully consider what *ethical* professional practice would look like in this situation. The International Visual Sociology Association's Code of Research Ethics and Guidelines for Visual Research spans multiple disciplines and certainly applies to the visual empirical research for theology that is outlined in this book.[5]

First, in the same way that a researcher would ask a gatekeeper for permission for participant observation, this request could mention that the researcher would like

---

[2]Gillian Rose. 2016. *Visual Methodologies: An Introduction to Researching with Visual Materials*, 4th edition. London: Sage, p. 363.

[3]See: Diana Papademas. 2009. 'IVSA Code of Research Ethics and Guidelines', *Visual Studies* 24 (3): 255.

[4]For GDPR guidelines, in the UK see the Information Commissioner's Office website: https://ico.org.uk/for-organisations/guide-to-data-protection/guide-to-the-general-data-protection-regulation-gdpr/ and in the EU https://gdpr-info.eu

[5]See: Diana Papademas. 2009. 'IVSA Code of Research Ethics and Guidelines', *Visual Studies* 24 (3): 250–7. The code is also available on the IVSA website: https://visualsociology.org/?page_id=405

to take photos. The consent form should include how long the empirical research will last and what events and venues will ideally be attended and photographed. The researcher should list what kinds of shots they envisage taking and in what contexts. If she will photograph live events, will she use a flash? Also, just as the gatekeeper would normally notify the people in their organization that a researcher will be in their midst over a period of time, so this notice should include that the researcher may take photographs. The information can include what parts of the gathering will be photographed, so that people can avoid these areas if they do not want to appear in a photograph. The information should also be clear about the purpose of the photographs, who will see them and how they will be used. It may be appropriate to include the contact details of the researcher, so that people can contact her with questions or concerns. A person may wish to look through the pictures to check whether they or their child ended up in the frame.

Second, although it may be *legal* to take photographs in public places, in order for your research to gain ethical clearance, you will need to consider what is actually *ethical* in these situations. How does obtaining consent work when photographing groups of people in a public place? The IVSA code states, 'Visual researchers may conduct research in public places or use publicly-available information about individuals (e.g., naturalistic observations in public places, analysis of public records, or archival research) without obtaining consent.'[6] However, according to the IVSA code, if photographs are taken via any form of communication or interaction, or involve some form of intervention, then consent should be requested in advance. It may be that even when formal consent for photography is obtained from a gatekeeper, informal consent should be obtained in the moment from the participants. In my own practice, I never photograph children without permission from their parents or guardians beforehand. As previously mentioned, with adults, if I've already taken a shot, I may feel that I should ask for permission to keep the picture. This is an issue that will need to be carefully navigated during fieldwork stages. It is normally best ethical practice that any kind of recording of participants requires informed consent, and this includes taking photographs. However, the IVSA code states that observations in public places whereby the resulting photographs are not anticipated to cause harm may be deemed to not require consent by an ethical clearance committee.[7]

Apart from crowd scenes, research may also include portraits or portrayals of small groups of people. In these cases, informed consent needs to be obtained.[8] Participants should be informed about the purpose of taking the photographs – will

---

[6]Ibid., p. 255.

[7]Ibid., p. 256.

[8]'Researchers obtain informed consent from research participants, students, employees, clients or others prior to photographing, videotaping, filming or recording them in any form, unless these activities involve simply naturalistic observations in public places and it is not anticipated that the recording will be used in a manner that could cause harm' (IVSA Code p. 256).

they be used for research analysis by the researcher alone? Or with a team? Or will they be used in presentations or publications? Navigating issues of confidentiality is also more complex when working with photographs that clearly portray individuals. One cannot promise anonymity for participants and then include photos of them in research reports. So, careful consideration of what kinds of photographs will be taken and how they will be used is important for the early stages of research. Also, consider what textual information will accompany any photographs used in publications.

Essentially, there is an ethical stance for visual research. Using an obvious camera and of course never taking covert photographs lends transparency to research practice in the field. There is also an ethical way of framing photographs, that does not omit visual data that might change the reading of the image. This extends to making sure that any caption that accompanies the publication of an image does not give misleading information about the context. When working with participant-provided or generated images, consent must be granted for the researcher to use these as visual data and presentations. The publication of images from research must have the consent of the image creators and the subjects. Personally, a prayerful respect for the dignity of research participants has helped to guide me when I encounter grey areas of ethical practice. For example, one participant who took photographs of what was significant to her, shared a (self-timed) photograph of herself and her boyfriend partially dressed in an embrace. This was quite important for my research because it opened up the space for a conversation about the importance of sex in the lives of students that otherwise I would not have broached. However, even though both she and her boyfriend said they were happy for me to use the photograph however I liked, I later chose not to, for the sake of protecting their modesty. Over the years I have usually found that I am more cautious on behalf of participants, than they are themselves.

In conclusion, the ethical issues surrounding visual material should not be ignored. However, they are easy enough to navigate so that they should not prevent the use of photographs in research. Careful research of national, cultural, local and institutional contexts in advance of research will aid in formulating a solid ethical clearance application and research proposal. It is worth remembering that research at its core demands a relationship of trust with participants, in order for real collaboration and partnership to work. This is the foundation for good ethical practice.[9]

---

[9]For further resources on visual research ethics, see Andrew Clark. 2012. 'Visual Ethics in a Contemporary Landscape', in Sarah Pink, ed. *Advances in Visual Methodologies*. Thousand Oaks, CA: Sage, pp. 17–36; Claudia Mitchell. 2011. 'Chapter 2: On a Pedagogy of Ethics in Visual Research: Who's in the Picture?', in *Doing Visual Research*. London: Sage, pp. 14–32; Andrew Clark. 2020. 'Visual Ethics beyond the Crossroads', in Luc Pauwels and Dawn Mannay, eds. *The Sage Handbook of Visual Research Methods*, 2nd edition. London: Sage, pp. 682–93; Melvin Delgado. 2015. *Urban Youth and Photovoice: Visual Ethnography in Action*. Oxford: Oxford University Press, pp. 146–75. Caroline C. Wang and Yanique A. Redwood-Jones. 2001. 'Photovoice Ethics: Perspectives from Flint Photovoice', *Health Education and Behavior* 28 (5): 560–72.

Analysing visual material

It may seem counterintuitive to be planning your approach to data analysis while you are still in the early stages of conceiving a project. However, it is hugely advisable to give careful consideration to this later stage of the project as early as possible, because having an idea about what kind of data you will need for your analysis shapes how you will gather the data. You should plan not only the subject areas to cover, but also what form (visual and/or textual, print and/or digital, etc.) your data should take. So, for example, an interview will normally yield three types of data: the fieldwork notes, the audio recording and the transcript. If you are using photographs, then you add visual data to audio and text. If the photographs are simply used as prompts within the interview, then they become text-based data via the transcript. But if your project generates visual material, it requires a process of analysis specific to itself.

In this chapter, I will introduce two approaches to visual analysis: content analysis and semiotics. However, I strongly advise reading more about methods of visual data analysis. Theo van Leeuwen and Carey Jewitt's edited *Handbook of Visual Analysis* is an excellent starting point for exploring a variety of approaches from different disciplinary perspectives.[10] Gillian Rose's book, *Visual Methodologies: An Introduction to the Interpretation of Visual Materials,* includes several chapters on different approaches to analysis, including compositional interpretation, content analysis, semiology, psychoanalysis and discourse analysis.[11] Overall, she argues for a 'critical approach' to interpreting visual material, which takes seriously the agency of the image to communicate. As we think about how to interpret photographs, it is worth keeping in mind her observation that 'visual imagery is never innocent; it is always constructed through various practices, technologies and knowledges.'[12]

Content analysis

Visual content analysis is the ostensibly simple technique of identifying what is portrayed within a photograph, and then counting those instances within a group of photographs. On the surface, this is an objective, quantitative analysis of observable phenomena. It entails a process very similar to coding a transcript. The researcher chooses what codes or specific themes to pay attention to within the pictures. Then, each photograph is looked at and codes are assigned. Philip Bell used content analysis to study how women have been portrayed in the media by studying the covers of the

---

[10]Theo van Leeuwen and Carey Jewitt, eds. 2001. *Handbook of Visual Analysis.* London: Sage.
[11]Gillian Rose. 2016. *Visual Methodologies: An Introduction to the Interpretation of Visual Materials,* 4th edition. London: Sage.
[12]Ibid., p. 56.

Australian magazine *Cleo* over twenty-five years. His work is typical of how content analysis is frequently used to study media trends using large numbers of images. He argues that this kind of analysis is almost impossible without a carefully defined hypothesis to guide the themes chosen for analysis.[13]

I disagree slightly, in that a grounded theory approach using a flexible hypothesis should open up space for discovering what is actually found within the photographs. It does entail the quantification of patterns through the coding of large numbers of photographs and counting particular codes. However, there may also be subtle patterns that can be discerned by the analysis. In this sense, content analysis is both quantitative and qualitative analysis. Thus, content analysis does not need to rely on pre-existing categories. Instead, new categories can emerge from the analysis, which avoids pre-emptive limiting of the findings. Gillian Rose explains that this more subjective analysis is why it is important to be explicitly reflexive, so that the findings convey how the content analysis happened in practice.[14]

The stages of a content analysis:

1 Gather the images
2 Devise categories and set up codes or 'descriptive labels'
3 Code in a way that is broadly replicable by someone else, adding codes as needed
4 Analyse the results

First, it is important to determine which photographs to use for this analysis. Because content analysis is often used as a way of comparing data, it is important to be analysing like with like. So, for example, if you are studying mass media images, do not mix these with participant-produced images. You may also wish to group photographs according to participant, so that all of one participant's images are analysed together as one unit, rather than each image analysed on its own. You may also wish to limit the number of photographs. I often asked participants to choose a picture that encapsulated the theme best for them, which meant I could focus on the analysis of only these photographs. You may also wish to use a sample of photographs, similar to other approaches to data sampling.

The second stage is to create codes of analysis. As mentioned above, this process is shaped by your research methodology and research focus. Regardless of whether you are using a clearly defined hypothesis or a slightly more open research question, you'll need to determine what sort of categories will be helpful for you when you draw conclusions based on your analysis. A code may apply to the entire photograph.

---

[13]Philip Bell. 2001. 'Content Analysis of Visual Images', in Theo van Leeuwen and Carey Jewitt, eds. *Handbook of Visual Analysis*. London: Sage, p. 13.
[14]Gillian Rose. 2016. *Visual Methodologies: An Introduction to the Interpretation of Visual Materials*, 4th edition. London: Sage, p. 136.

For example, one might count the number of landscape scenes or images depicting friendship. Individual items within the photograph may be analysed, so that it is possible that multiple codes may co-exist within an image. Ideally the creation of codes should facilitate a systematic approach that can be applied to a large number of photographs.

For example, in my own early research, I studied the images students in Kyiv put on their walls. I performed a content analysis of the photographs that I had taken of my participants' walls. Initially, I looked through the photographs and noted the various types of images depicted within the photographs. I followed Bell's method for performing a content analysis by organizing the codes according to variables and values.[15] For him, a variable is the name of a range of options. For example, the gender or age of a person pictured. The value is the category within that option, which in this example would be female/male or child/adult. The variable and values to analyse are chosen according to the research question. Are you interested in the possible different responses between women and men? Old and young? Depending on the research question, breaking the categories down into variables and values helps to complexify the codes. For example, one of my variables was 'person', and I only coded for this variable if an image on a student wall contained a person. I then further analysed this using the values of pop celebrity, sports star, saint, friend/family, politician, unknown.[16]

Third, once these categories or variables/values are set up, one works through all of the photographs, assigning codes. You can create custom-made charts or use spreadsheets. Most qualitative data analysis software will allow you to work with images and the advantage is that you may have codes that cross over with the text-based analysis that you are doing. At this stage, think about the reliability of your analysis. 'Reliability' refers to the consistency of your coding. If you were to code the same photos on a different occasion, would the results be the same? Or, if someone else were given the same categories and looked at the same images, would they code them in the same way?

Finally, the results are then compared and tested across variables. This is most often done by counting the frequency of an occurrence of a code. These can be compared between variables, if your research focus is asking this sort of question of the data. Once the contents have been documented, the next step is to consider the actual

---

[15]Philip Bell. 2001. 'Content Analysis of Visual Images', in Theo van Leeuwen and Carey Jewitt, eds. *Handbook of Visual Analysis*. London: Sage, pp. 15–20.
[16]For other examples, Carlo Nardella's study is typical of how visual content analysis is often used for media studies, see: 2012. 'Religious Symbols in Italian Advertising: Symbolic Appropriation and the Management of Consent', *Journal of Contemporary Religion* 27 (2): 217–40. Roman Williams used visual content analysis in his study of participant-provided images within a congregation, see his 2019 article: 'Engaging and Researching Congregations Visually: Photovoice in a Mid-Sized Church', *Ecclesial Practices* 6: 5–27. https://doi.org/10.1163/22144471-00601002

significance of what has been found. Thus, a good content analysis requires another pass in the later stages of analysis to ask 'what is theologically significant about these findings?' This requires a shift from quantitative analysis towards the qualitative task of interpretation and explanation.

Semiotics

Whilst content analysis *counts* what is seen, semiotics digs deeper into *interpreting* what is seen. The two approaches can be used together – semiotics helps us to identify what we see; content analysis provides a system for quantifying it. Semiotics is qualitative analysis; content analysis is (mostly) quantitative.

Semiotics is essentially the study of signs or symbols. Within this field of study, the term 'sign' indicates a basic unit of language or image. Analysis reveals that each sign consists of two parts: the signified and the signifier. The signified is the concept or object (e.g. a very young human) and the signifier is the sound or image that is attached to the signified (e.g. baby). The actual object in the world that the sign is related to is the 'referent'.[17] Thus, semiotics is the study of how symbols come to have meaning. In recognition that it is people and cultures who invest symbols with meaning, this approach has developed into what is called 'social semiotics'.

Jewitt and Oyama offer three types of meaning that emerge from a social semiotic analysis of visual material.[18] First, *representational* meaning is conveyed via the basic material that is shown in the image, whether this tells a story or conveys concepts. Second, an image may be analysed for its *interactive* meaning, which is how the image creates a relationship between the viewer and what is pictured within the frame. The factors that affect this interplay are distance, (eye) contact and point of view. Finally, a photograph or any image contains *compositional* meaning. For example, the location of the subject, whether in the centre, left side or top of the frame, affects how the meaning is read. The framing of the subject affects how the image connects or disconnects the pictured elements. Salience refers to how eye-catching a particular object may be, which causes it to catch the eye or be overlooked.

Social semiotics employs the term 'modality' to refer to the level of representing a sign as true or real. Those who read a message judge how factual or fictional it is. Thus, judging the modality of an image is not so much about whether it is showing something real but more the degree to which it is represented as true.[19] So, a unit of

---

[17]Gillian Rose. 2016. *Visual Methodologies: An Introduction to the Interpretation of Visual Materials*, 4th edition. London: Sage, p. 166.

[18]Carey Jewitt and Rumiko Oyama. 2001. 'Visual Meaning: A Social Semiotic Approach', in Theo van Leeuwen and Carey Jewitt, eds. *Handbook of Visual Analysis*. London: Sage, pp. 134–56.

[19]Gunther Kress and Theo van Leeuwen. 2006. *Reading Images: The Grammar of Visual Design*, 2nd edition. London: Routledge, pp. 154–5.

visual analysis might be to judge whether the photograph aims to be naturalistic or is quite obviously staged or otherwise manipulated. This does not mean that what is pictured is does not represent reality, but that the meanings are filtered through an artificial lens. This is a judgement that can be made by a viewer and of course by the researcher as part of visual analysis. However, it seems to me, that a key component of modality is the intention and context of the photographer. Thus, the story behind the photograph is a central component of this type of analysis. The modality of the image may reveal the photographer's perception of reality.

Alternatively, when planning your analysis, you may find it helpful to follow what van Leeuwen refers to as 'Barthian visual semiotics', which entails simply separating out two layers of meanings within an image.[20] First, determine what three-dimensional object is *denoted* in a two-dimensional photograph. Second, draw out any *connotative* meanings. This entails working out what ideas, values and concepts may be represented by the people, places and things pictured within a photograph. On the other hand, van Leeuwen also describes what he calls an 'iconography approach', which reads images on three different levels. The first is *representational*, quite similar to 'denoted' described above. The second is a *conventional* level of meaning, which entails reading images as they are meant to be read by the creator. The third level of meaning is *intuitional* in that it interprets what is seen in ways that may not have been intended by the photographer but nevertheless may be a valid reading.[21]

Thus, semiology is a highly interpretive approach to analysing visual material. If you, as the researcher, are the one doing the semiotic analysis, then it will be highly important to be explicitly transparent and reflexive about the presuppositions and theological convictions that are guiding your interpretation. It will be important to separate your own interpretation from those of your participants. If you intend to involve participants in drawing out these layers of meaning, then you will want to work this into your interview questions or add a stage of participative analysis. Oliffe et al. have written a helpful account of how they analysed participant-produced photographs in their study of fatherhood and smoking.[22] They analysed the photographs taken by fathers of new babies in four levels. First, they did a 'Preview', which entailed viewing each photograph alongside the accompanying interview. They created notes from the interview to accompany each photograph, thus privileging and connecting the interpretations of participants to the images. Second, they did a 'Review' of all the images, adding their own interpretations and readings to the participants' perspectives. Third, they performed a 'Cross-Photo Comparison',

---

[20]See: Theo van Leeuwen. 2001. 'Semiotics and Iconography', in Theo van Leeuwen and Carey Jewitt, eds. *Handbook of Visual Analysis*. London: Sage, pp. 94–100.

[21]Ibid., pp. 100–18. Van Leeuwen was drawing on the work of art historian Erwin Panofsky. I write about how Panofsky's semiotics was used in ministry in Chapter 7 of this book.

[22]See John L. Oliffe, Joan L. Bottorff, Mary Kelly and Michael Halpin. 2008. 'Analyzing Participant Produced Photographs from an Ethnographic Study of Fatherhood and Smoking', *Research in Nursing and Health* 31: 529–39.

viewing all of the photographs in mass and then dividing them into categories and then groups. Their final stages, 'Theorizing', involved connecting their categories and groups to theories from relevant literature. 'The purpose of theorizing was to develop a more abstract understanding by linking each of the inductively-derived empirically-based categories to theoretically informed study findings.'[23] Thus, in addition to gathering rich data and thick description, the photographs were also used to resource further layers of analysis, enabling the expansion of what was initially interpreted within the visual material.

Conclusion

In conclusion, it seems to me that both research ethics and data analysis should be linked to one's vocation. A deep desire to serve people should lead to a commitment to carefully planned ethical practice. And gazing upon an image for analysis need not be entirely a scientific activity, as it may at times feel it is reduced to by social researchers. Instead, it seems to me that we can draw on centuries of Christian tradition in reading icons. Not the 'iconography' mentioned above and used by those in the field of semiotics. Instead, I refer to the Christian practice of gazing upon a religious icon as a spiritual act. The icons direct us toward a reality beyond ourselves. The saints and Jesus exist in the heavenly realm and gaze out at the viewer. Thus, looking goes two ways, we see the icons and at the same time are seen. We can approach reading photographs with a similar stance. Just as God grants the power of the eyes of the mind to recognise something of God in the icon, and in the same way we rely on the Spirit of God to analyse our pictures. This approach requires a humbling of the self before the photograph in order to really see something of God's work and nature. In this way, seeing may turn into a sense of being seen, of new possibilities, of being drawn into engagement with the world portrayed. We will explore these themes further in the final three chapters of this book.

---

[23]Ibid., p. 536.

Part II

Doing Ministry with Photographs

7

Photographs as a Ministry Tool

This second section of the book considers how work with photographs may be fruitful within ministry practice. I have observed a fluidity between employing photographs within research and ministry. Some students who have found research with photographs generative have, once in ministry, turned to using them within different aspects of their practice. Some of the examples in this chapter began as research projects and became ministry activities. In this chapter, I give multiple examples of how photographs can be used within ministry practice to resource strategy, ministry activities and discipleship. Then, Chapter 8 considers how photographs can resource theological reflection, which is increasingly recognized as an essential skill for supporting innovative, spiritually sensitive ministry. Chapter 9 focuses on how photographs can be used within personal spiritual practices. In a sense, we are turning from using photographs in a manufactured research environment towards how they can resource everyday life and ministry. Typical of much of practical theology, the lines are blurred in some cases between research and ministry.

Icons have been described as windows into heaven. They are a form of visual theology, objects for private and corporate prayer. In this chapter, I will argue that using photographs within ministry also opens up windows. These may or may not offer vistas into the heavenly realms. But the photographs will give us views into other people's lives and even, as Mark Oestreicher observes below, into their souls. Bob Orsi wrote about religion as a web of relationships between heaven and earth.[1] Many people are part of these networks and, as Orsi argues, we 'get caught up in these bonds, whether we want to or not'. We can get so caught up in our own interpretations, that we forget to include the others who are part of this network, including God, historical figures and the people among whom we worship. We have in-built normativities, ways of deciding what is good or bad ministry. One of the key advantages of using photographs within ministry is that it gives everyone a voice into the theologies being formed and practiced.

---

[1]Bob Orsi. 2005. *Between Heaven and Earth: The Religious Worlds People Make and the Scholars Who Study Them*. Princeton, NJ: Princeton University Press, p. 5.

Below I give examples of different ways that photographs have been used in ministry. This is not intended to be an exhaustive list, but instead to represent a variety of approaches. I'll start with a photo documentary approach, then photo elicitation with an archive and conclude with narrated photography approaches.

Photo documentary approach

In his article advocating visual methods for studying churches, Richter mentioned the 'Vicinity Walk' which entails going around the environs of a church and observing buildings, greenspaces, areas of growth and decline, etc. He notes that the camera can be used to aid this process, leading to a more detailed sense of the local physical and social environment.[2] It seems to me that this approach could be used by a local congregation to explore what it means for their church to be situated where it is. Using a camera gives the photographer a different kind of attentiveness. Richter writes, 'The photographer must choose what, and what not, to photograph and what to include in, or exclude from, the limited frame of the photograph. The camera's optics may help the researcher see the vicinity better than with the naked eye ...' (p. 209) Indeed, if undertaken with a spirit of curiosity and an eye for detail, the process itself of photographing the geographic context of a church or parish will yield new insights. A group reflection on the process and on the photographs themselves can be highly generative, yielding new insights for the vision of a church's role in the local community.

In 2008, the diocese of London and the Church Mission Society collaborated to create a new children and youth ministry resource for Easter.[3] Dennis Morris, a photographer who toured with the Sex Pistols and is known for his pictures of Bob Marley, was commissioned to work with a youth group to recreate scenes from the passion of Christ. Together they explored the Easter story, using their own bodies and physical environs to create six tableaus which were photographed by Morris. The project, 'Easter Images', resulted in unusual depictions of six key events of the story: Palm Sunday, the Last Supper, Gethsemane, the Trial, the Crucifixion and the Resurrection. The idea was not to represent what these events mean to young people, but instead to show what the event would have looked like within the contemporary cultural context of North London. Morris explained, 'I wanted to give a spontaneous feel and quality to each photo. I focused on ensuring that each of them looked like it wasn't too set or staged, I was going for a snapshot feel, immediacy,

---

[2]Philip Richter. 2011. 'Different Lenses for Studying Local Churches – a Critical Study of the Uses of Photographic Research Methods', *Journal of Contemporary Religion* 26: 207–23. http://dx.doi.org/10.1080/13537903.2011.57 3335

[3]https://jonnybaker.blogs.com/jonnybaker/2008/02/shooting-jesus.html viewed 8 December 2022.

Figure 7.1 'The Crucifixion'. Photograph by Dennis Morris. The copyright for the Easter 2008 images is held jointly by Dennis Morris, the Diocese of London and CMS. Used with permission.

capturing a moment in time.'[4] Bob Mayo, who worked with Morris, youth leader Ben Bell and the young people, reflected on the process:

> Jesus going to his death forlorn and alone is the ultimate example of something seemingly hopeless but actually fabulous. In our small way this is what we experienced during our week together. We were immersed in the Easter story and the process of our taking the photographs began to run parallel to some of the events of Holy Week. The young people came to be photographed largely out of loyalty to Ben but they did not fully understand the significance of what we were trying to achieve. At the Last Supper, I imagine the attitude of the disciples to have been somewhat similar. Jesus would have bemused them; they would have known that something important was going on but not quite sure what it was. We were concerned when we realized that the young people would be coming straight from school, but then the poignancy of the school uniforms in the images cemented in our minds the ordinariness of the disciples as the key players in the drama of Holy Week. Dennis was creating new ways of looking at what would otherwise have been familiar, ordinary and drab.[5]

Being involved in this activity caused the young people involved to translate the Easter story into their own lives.

---

[4]Philip Richter. 2017. *Spirituality in Photography*. London: Darton, Longman & Todd, p. 53.
[5]The photographs can viewed here: https://www.london.anglican.org/mission/childrens-ministry/easter-2008/ viewed 8 December 2022.

This photography project has high ministry value in itself for the experience that the young people and their leaders had while doing it. However, another outcome, of course, was the photographs that were produced. Morris said, 'I hope these images will provoke thought and generate discussion around the significance of Easter.'[6] Mayo, who created a resource pack to accompany the distribution of the photographs to youth leaders, reflects, 'Research with young people has shown that images like these can be a wonderful stimulus for open-ended discussion on themes of spirituality and meaning. Images appeal to the imagination of children and young people as well as to their thinking and feeling selves. Images provide space to wonder and to explore, without the tyranny of being expected to come up with the right answer.'[7] Essentially, the pictures served to translate the Easter story into a specific contemporary context, which can then ignite the theological imagination of other viewers.

Photo elicitation with an archive

There are many examples of photo elicitation with an archive being used for a variety of ministries outside of the research interview or focus group. Some of these developed because those in ministry recognized that images help people to consider issues side-on. For example, St Clare's Cathedral has produced an archive of images to support people leading contemplative prayer sessions.[8] These cards are called 'Gazing Prayers' and consist of a variety of images of people, places and objects. The cards are laid out on the floor, or a low table, and people are invited to allow their prayers to be directed by the pictures as they gaze upon them. Those who created the archive reflect, 'Sometimes we struggle to know how to pray, and words can seem limiting or inadequate. Gazing Prayers help us to open our hearts and minds to the prompting of the Holy Spirit.' Romans 8.26 is quoted, 'we do not know how to pray as we ought, but the Spirit intercedes with sighs too deep for words.' It seems to me that the photographs bypass words and enable those praying with an openness to the Spirit of God to connect with the themes pictured.

Along similar lines, Mark Oestreicher published an archive called *Every Picture Tells a Story: 48 Evocative Photographs for Inspiring Reaction and Reflection* [See Figure 3.1], created for use within youth ministry.[9] The black-and-white professional

---

[6]http://news.bbc.co.uk/1/hi/england/london/7300089.stm viewed 8 December 2022.
[7]https://www.london.anglican.org/mission/childrens-ministry/easter-2008/ viewed 8 December 2022.
[8]'Gazing Prayers' cards produced by St Clare's at the Cathedral: https://stclaresatthecathedral.org/2018/05/16/gazing-prayers/ [accessed 27 September 2022].
[9]Mark Oestreicher. 2002. *Every Picture Tells a Story: 48 Evocative Photographs for Inspiring Reaction and Reflection*. Grand Rapids, MI: Zondervan/Youth Specialities. In 2013 a digital edition with new photographs and a leaders guide was published by The Youth Cartel, LLC. www.theyouthcartel.com

photographs were designed to span a range of moods. Their primary use is to be laid out on a table and used as discussion starters. Oestreicher reflects that in the years since they were first published, the photographs have supported all ages of participants for looking 'inward and verbalizing what they're sensing or feeling or thinking or hearing from God'.[10] Promotional material describes the photographs as relying upon 'the undeniable evocative force of black-and-white photographs to birth reactions and reflection' which 'opens up new doorways into your students' souls'. This is a bold claim, but it chimes with what we have heard elsewhere about discovering that photographs can function as windows into the spiritual side of life. Indeed, Oestreicher contextualizes the use of the photographs within the youth spirituality movement, which entails connecting contemporary forms of ministry with ancient Christian practices, helping young people to practice scriptural meditation, spiritual listening and experiments with silence. For him, the photographs are fuel for encouraging contemplative practice among young people who have little experience with this kind of prayer. Describing this process in the book, he relates that he advises participants to choose a photograph that speaks to them, and then, while gazing at it, to ask:

> What do I see beyond this photo? How can I see the reflection of God in this photo? What does this photo remind me of in my own story? What deeper meaning can I find in this photo – especially a meaning that resonates with my spiritual longings or frustrations or questions or complacency? When I look at these pictures, I pray, 'God, what are you doing in my life? Where are you present and active, and how can these pictures point me to that reality? How can these snapshots capture or leverage or mirror the work you're doing in me?'[11]

For him, the photographs are central to this practice because of the narrative power of images and their potential for igniting the theological imagination. Oestreicher reflects, 'Black-and-white photos are pregnant with story. They beg the imagination to kick into high gear. I find God's story, my story, and many other stories in these images – especially when I look at them contemplatively.'[12]

Archives have also been used in evangelism – the practice of sharing the Christian faith with others. For example, Cru, a student ministry based in the United States, uses a series of fifty photographs called 'Soularium'. The creator, Leigh Ann Dull, says that 'Art has purpose from God's design. One of those purposes is to open people's hearts and minds, to open the shutters of their heart to a Creator.'[13] The pack of postcard-sized coloured photographs is intended to be shown to another person, who is then invited

---

[10]Ibid., p. 4.
[11]Ibid., p. 8.
[12]Ibid.
[13]https://www.cru.org/us/en/communities/locations/americas/united-states/nyc-art-residency.html viewed 8 February 2023.

to choose three images to describe his or her life right now. Follow-up questions are asked, such as, 'Choose an image that relates to your spiritual state right now.' Then the person can be asked, 'What does each image represent about your life?' The aim is to draw out a person's story to enable the listener to discern connections with their own story or the Christian story. A promotional video observes, 'Just as sunlight illuminates a solarium, Soularium opens a window to the soul.' Here again we see this observation that the photographs are opening up spaces for spiritual engagement. A Soularium training guide states, 'Something unique happens when we look at an image. It conjures up associations that are as unique as we are. Our experience shapes what we see.'[14] So the pictures are used to link a person's memories and emotional history to a conversation about their own spiritual journey.

I spoke with a staff member from Cru's UK branch, 'Agape', who regularly uses the Soularium archive within her evangelism when connecting with students in public spaces. She said that she loves using this tool because it's more fun and engaging than an interview style evangelistic survey. Talking about the photographs creates an open space for a response – without being completely open ended. Sometimes the question about where they are spiritually is something they haven't thought about before, but the pictures give them categories and a means of response.[15] The only drawback, in her eyes, is that one needs to find space to lay out the images, which can be a challenge in some venues. In one such location, she decided to try asking the questions without the photos. She recounted that it fell flat because the questions really needed the pictures. In her opinion, choosing the photograph gave students a deeper connection with the question. The image may be chosen because of the visual information it contains, but it functions to connect a person to the emotions and experiences behind the question. She now uses a pin board to display the photographs.

Another staff member from Agape who has used the photos in conversations with students for more than ten years, observed that some students are more adept at relating the photographs to the question posed than others. He noted that particularly student engineers and mathematicians tended to want to give a quite literal reading of the photos and would struggle to engage if a picture did not exactly portray their

---

[14]https://www.cru.org/us/en/train-and-grow/share-the-gospel/outreach-strategies/soularium/how-to-use-soularium.html viewed on 7 December 2022. Their website states, 'Because images connect deeply with our emotions and experiences, they enable us to engage in meaningful conversations about life & God.' https://www.cru.org/us/en/train-and-grow/share-the-gospel/outreach-strategies/soularium.html viewed on 7 December 2022. Cru has also developed a digital resource called 'Backstory' that uses narrative and images to share the gospel. https://crustore.org/product/backstory-life-large-revisited-ebook/

[15]She also said that she sometimes uses these prompts: 'Pick an image that describes your ideal world, your world as it is, and why do you think your ideal world is not your real world.' She observes that this is helpful for talking about issues of sin. It's a way of enabling people to articulate their own notion of sin within their own worldview. She says that sometimes she might also ask, 'Which image can represent a solution? To help you reach your ideal life?' She loves this approach because she says it is a way of conveying the hope of the Christian gospel without using Christian words.

response. He has now been commissioned to develop a UK context version of the deck of thirty-five photographs.[16] The new archive incorporates photographs that may elicit a range of emotional responses and convey a variety of scenes for the more literal reading. He notes that Agape is very passionate about using photographs to connect with students because talking about photographs helps them to talk about personal spirituality, since the focus is on the picture, rather than their private life. Agape and the wider Cru community believe that this approach is one of their most valuable resources.

In another example, Jon Marlow, in his work to support missional activities for a Church of England diocese, used an archive of photographic postcards to draw out the missional impulses of participants.[17] The aim was to give voice to the intuited knowledge of the local people to resource church leaders' missional strategy for a geographic region. The photographs were intentionally ambiguous images, most taken by Marlow, with the rest used under Creative Commons licenses and downloaded from a range of image-sharing websites. Of the forty-six images, fourteen could be read as a metaphor for a biblical concept, ten pictured church buildings, nine showed metaphors for growth and eighteen contained people of a variety of ages. Working with multiple local groups, participants were asked to choose a postcard to answer each question: 'What is important to you about your church?', 'What do you see God doing in and through your church at the moment?' and 'What do you think God might be calling you to as a church in the next five years?' Each person wrote their answers on the back of the postcard, but also verbally shared their answers with the group. The session was recorded, and, at the end, the cards were collected for analysis.

Marlow notes that this was a highly successful method for creating collaborative and creative missional strategies for a region. In this case, a surprising finding was that people often had a longing to increase the diversity of their local church but had not previously vocalized this. Consistently across the diocese, the most popular image was one showing five arms belonging to people of different races. Each hand holds their neighbour's wrist to form a circle (Figure 7.2, below). From the 2,763 postcards selected during the repetitions of this exercise in different locations, this image was chosen 156 times, which was unexpected given the almost totally homogenous ethno-racial make-up of the church communities who took part.

This example demonstrates how photo-elicitation can be used to open up a question rather than lead participants into a predictable response. From the data, we see that there were various interpretations of this particular image: 'It is multi-racial, inviting to everyone', 'We are all working together to keep our church ecumenical.'

---

[16]It is called 'Unfilter'd'. There are other decks that have been developed for other contexts, including Russia, China and Italy.

[17]Jon Marlow and Sarah Dunlop. 2021. 'Answers on a Postcard: Photo Elicitation in the Service of Local Ecclesial Strategy', *Ecclesial Practices* 8 (2): 165–84. https://doi.org/10.1163/22144471-bja10014

Figure 7.2 The front and back of postcards used for photo-elicitation. Photograph by John Marlow. Used with permission. Source: 'Diversity' by Wonder Woman 0721. Licensed under Creative Commons 2.0. Available: https://www.flickr.com/photos/wildrose115/27623264486.

We have to hold on tight to each other' and '[We are] connected and part of a group in a welcoming environment'. The process of working with photographs on postcards enabled an intuited, operant missional drive to become explicit. Thus, the photographs were key to creating the democratization of local and regional Mission Action Plans. Marlow was able to take these expressions of ordinary theology and place them into dialogue with the normative theologies of the Diocesan mission strategy statement and other Church of England missional statements.

Narrated photography approach

Within the Church of England in the UK, Ministry Division has devised a new protocol to support people as they discern a vocation to ordained ministry. Stage one of this 'Shared Discernment Process' entails six interviews each with an assessor. In four of these meetings, the candidate is invited to use images, objects, video or music as they discuss their vocation, faith, pastoral ministry or communication of the gospel.[18] This technique is recommended because it is generally seen as a helpful way of opening up a quality conversation in the brief time that assessors have with candidates. Marlow, in his role as a Diocesan Director of Ordinands (DDO), often

---

[18]See https://www.churchofengland.org/life-events/vocations/preparing-ordained-ministry/understanding-discernment viewed 5 December 2022.

invites candidates to bring a black-and-white photograph they have taken that describes 'how you are hearing from God at the moment' and another 'that describes your vocation'. He argues that although narrated photography is the central aspect of this process, what may be overlooked is that if the visual material generated were subjected to a fuller analysis, even deeper levels of meaning are created for both the candidate and the DDO.[19] With this in mind, he uses his knowledge of semiotics to resource how he uses the photographs. Drawing on the work of art historian Erwin Panofsky, he looks for three levels of meaning within a visual sign. First, the 'natural reading' is observing the basic details, indeed, what might be counted within a content analysis. Second, the 'conventional reading' entails interpreting the image in full awareness of one's own and the creator's context. Third, the image may be analysed at the level of 'intuition', which looks for a meaning within the image that may not have been consciously intended by the photographer. He uses the images with groups of candidates as intended, to open up spaces for exploring issues of faith and vocation. But, taking this further, with Panofsky's third level in mind, he asks candidates 'what do you see in this image that you hadn't intended to capture?' He argues that an image can be the bearer of theological truth when the various levels of meanings are negotiated through discussion and awareness of the reception of the image. He refers to these as the 'perfume of meanings' that accompany the image.

Multiple layers of meanings were also evident when Henk de Roest spent nearly a year with a Dutch church congregation that was closing their building. Due to budget cuts, the denomination has decided to merge two congregations and close one of the church buildings. After careful negotiation with the church leaders, de Roest was given permission to do a case study project with the congregation. He called this a 'photo-reflection' approach, because the participants were invited to add written or oral comments to photographs that they had taken or pictures from a third party.[20] He asked people to choose pictures (a scene, an object, a part of the building) that showed what they will miss most when the building is closed down. In group sessions, they were invited to tell the group what the photograph means to them. He then carefully analysed the images and text, developing codes and then devising integrating concepts that connected them. The analysis of the photographs and accompanying texts revealed that the church building was highly meaningful to people particularly when it performed a dual role – 'a common place to connect with God and each other'.[21] The research outcomes resourced knowledge around the nature

---

[19]Jon Marlow. 2022. 'Unlocking Deeper Levels of Theological Meaning from Visual Data', a paper delivered on 2 March 2022 at St Augustine's College Research Seminar.

[20]The photographs were not used to draw out responses within an interview, so he distinguished his approach from photo elicitation. See: Hendrik Pieter de Roest. 2013. '"Losing a Common Space to Connect": An Inquiry into Inside Perspectives on Church Closure Using Visual Methods', *International Journal of Practical Theology* 17 (2): 292–313. Personally, I would still call this a photo elicitation approach, because the photographs were used during the group sessions to draw out comment.

[21]Ibid., p. 307.

of meaningful attachment to a church building and formed the key component of a guide that de Roest wrote for pastors about how to manage church building closure.

However, the activities of the project also served to support the congregation through the process of grieving the loss of the building. De Roest observed that group pastoral care occurred via the group meetings where emotions were shared, memories and photographs exchanged, and stories told.

> It requires ample time and a safe space in which to share and cherish what has been valuable. This communal pastoral care made grief less 'harsh' or 'sharp'. A church closure does indeed threaten to destroy the fabric of the social and spiritual life of the congregation. Yes, the process of taking and picking pictures, commenting on them and talking about them, offered the participants a stimulus toward a process of recovery. The building was lost, but there may have been a community regained.[22]

He observed that the photographs served as vessels, in which people could place their meanings, knowledge, memories and experiences. They also functioned like windows into the world of the congregation members, making them accessible to others. The pictures also functioned like an alternative language, transcending verbal expressions.

Henk de Roest's photo reflection project is a hybrid between a research project and a ministry activity. His findings about people's emotional investment in a church building contribute to knowledge about theories of place attachment, which most often focus on domestic spaces. His work also served to question some of the theological metaphors that the central denomination employed to facilitate the building closure, for example drawing on Psalm 84 as calling people to be 'God's people on the move'. This 'placelessness' theology of church was in direct conflict with the finding that people had a psychological need for a sacred and communal space as part of their journey of discipleship. The project gave voice to the people, which in turn could then be used to reform denominational strategy and communication. Finally, of course, the activities of the project became examples of the shape that group 'transitional pastoral care' might fruitfully take.

Roman Williams explored whether engagement with a topic could be increased if a congregation does a narrated photography type of project together.[23] Working with a group from a church congregation in Midwestern United States, he led a series of three sessions that aimed to help congregation members to think about what the church needs to do in order to cultivate intergenerational relationships. The sixty participants were invited to take part in three different photography activities over the three weeks of the sessions. They interacted in small groups with the photographs

---

[22]Ibid., pp. 312–13

[23]Roman Williams. 2019. 'Engaging and Researching Congregations Visually: Photovoice in a Mid-Sized Church', *Ecclesial Practices* 6: 5–27. https://doi.org/10.1163/22144471-00601002

that others had taken. Williams observed that, similar to de Roest's reflections above, when a group thinks critically about shared experiences using photographs, they build relationships. This then results in a raised awareness of the shared concerns and needs within the group. He also observed that telling stories with and around photographs gave congregation members the opportunity to see their own context through the eyes of someone else. This brought people from different backgrounds and demographics together around shared meanings, but also led to empathetic listening. This afforded the 'opportunity for a relatively voiceless group (or peoples' unvoiced concerns) to shed light on challenges, needs, and/or injustices as a step toward social change'.[24] This then empowered people to articulate (either visually or using stories) evidence-based arguments about the situation. Thus, congregation members were owning the outcomes of the process and equipped to do so again around another issue. The church leaders embraced the outcomes of the project, displaying the photographs and accompanying textual comments in the church building, even including comments that were critical of the church. One church member remarked that seeing the church through the perspective of other congregation members was deeply provocative and instructive.

Conclusion

I hope this chapter has not only recounted ways of using photographs within ministry but will be generative of ministry innovation. Just as Douglas Harper argued that photographs expand the possibilities for sociology,[25] I hope I have demonstrated here that photographs expand the possibilities for ministry. We saw in the work of Marlow, de Roest and Williams how ministry with photographs can be inclusive and collaborative, leading to a democratization of the theologies that emerge. Ministry activities with photographs speak to people's souls and minds. And the photographs produced create visual forms of theology that uniquely convey the lived theologies that are operant within a community.

Oestreicher wrote that photographs open new doorways into the soul and Cru use their archive Soularium for this very reason. Indeed, similar to icons, they function as windows into heaven or the spiritual realm. As doorways or windows, they open up new spaces for wonder and insight. Photographs invite the viewer to see differently, perhaps through another's eyes. Jeffery Samuels invited Buddhist monks to photograph what was beautiful in their spiritual practices and discovered

---

[24]Ibid., p. 10.
[25]Douglas Harper. 1988. 'Visual Sociology: Expanding Sociological Vision', *The American Sociologist* 19 (Spring): 54–70. https://jan.ucc.nau.edu/~pms/cj355/readings/harper.pdf

that their responses 'broke' his own frame of reference.[26] Breaking may not sound comfortable, and as we work with photographs, we can discover that they expose our own preconceptions and invite us to see differently. This is a humbling activity but is highly generative. And, as we've seen evidenced above, builds bridges of shared meaning between people. In the next two chapters, we will continue to explore how photographs take us out of our taken-for-granted meanings when we draw them into our theological reflection and spiritual practices.

---

[26]Jeffery Samuels. 2004. 'Breaking the Ethnographer's Frames: Reflections on the Use of Photo Elicitation in Understanding Sri Lankan Monastic Culture', *American Behavioral Scientist* 47 (12): 1528–50.

8

Photographs and
Theological Reflection

In the previous chapter, I made a case for how photographs can open up spaces for encounter within Christian ministry. In this chapter, I explore how the theological imagination may be ignited using photographs, leading to deeper possibilities for theological reflection. I will explore how Killen and De Beer's model of theological reflection centralized the use of images within the reflective process. I'll explain how my own work with visual material revealed how people process faith and life – doing 'theological reflection' unconsciously. Finally, the chapter includes three examples of how others have used photographs within theological reflection, and how this has resourced their ministry practice.

First, however, I offer a definition of 'theological reflection'. By this, I mean the intentional and intuited process of learning and meaning-making in relation to everyday life and experiences of the Divine other. It is a core aspect of discipleship and spiritual growth. Reflection occurs as people learn through considering their experiences in light of their culture, faith tradition, other experiences, studies, intuition and many other sources, assigning the sources different values according to their authority and reliability. This 'sense-making' then goes on to inform how a person will react to new situations. This reflection is theological when it is faith seeking understanding, so that the eyes of faith are applied to the process of meaning-making. Instead of being limited to questions such as 'What should I do?' and 'What does my tribe think about this situation?' the movement goes further and asks 'How might God see this situation?' and 'How has my tradition informed other people with these experiences?' and 'What have I learned about God?' All people of faith practice theological reflection in some form, and, whether it is intentional and well-researched or messy and ambiguous, it is a spiritually sensitive and an attentive process of making sense of life in light of faith.[1]

---

[1]This is further explored here: Sarah Dunlop, Catherine Nancekievill, and Pippa Ross-McCabe. 2021. 'Exploring the Reflective Practice of Anglican Laity: Finding Manna in the Desert', *Practical Theology* 14 (4): 309–22. https://www.tandfonline.com/doi/full/10.1080/1756073X.2021.1957074

Engaging the theological imagination

I propose that a key reason why photographs can be so generative for theological reflection is because they create spaces for engaging the theological imagination. By 'theological imagination' I mean an intuited sense of the Divine that emerges through curiosity about what could be, rather than direct experience about what is. Much has been written on the topic of the theological imagination, and my aim is not to recount that discourse here, but rather to draw out how imagination relates to theological reflection with photographs. C. S. Lewis argues that the imagination is key to meaning-making.[2] The imagination is more than how we learn and know. It is also how we make connections between things that might otherwise appear wholly separated. It enables an intuited sense of the relationship between ideas and images to emerge and take shape. Unlike reasoned thinking, the imagination may be working subconsciously, working out possibilities and connections in the midst of other activities.

Development psychologist Paul Harris has studied the importance of imaginative play for children's development in engaging with the world around them. He argues that real-world experiences resource a child's play, and the imagination enables them to extrapolate this into other related scenarios, which may then help unfamiliar situations to become manageable. His research demonstrated that the imagination is vital for making sense of reality, and it is not just playing with mere fantasies.[3] It seems to me that a person of any age can use their imagination to 'play with' experiences of the Divine in everyday life and use this to create theologies that encapsulate their spiritual learning and reflection. The very act of having faith and growing as a disciple is to use our imagination to 'see' and sense the Divine in everyday life. Growing in knowledge of the transcendent God requires the theological imagination because it is not limited to what can be experienced and seen.

Moving beyond epistemological questions towards considering the very nature of being human, James K. A. Smith, referred to in the introduction, charts an anthropology which emphasizes that human persons 'are not primarily thinking things … We are embodied, affective creatures … '[4] Smith is making the case for how worship functions within the lived experiences of people of faith. But what is interesting for this chapter is his view of people as 'affective creatures' with imaginations, not primarily thinking beings. Along these lines, Amos Yong, writing about communicating faith essentials to people with Down syndrome, observes:

---

[2]Clive Staples Lewis. 1979. 'Blusphels and Flalanferes', in Walter Hooper, ed. *Selected Literary Essays*. Cambridge: Cambridge University Press, p. 265.
[3]Paul Harris. 2000. *The Work of the Imagination*. Oxford: Wiley-Blackwell.
[4]James K. A. Smith. 2009. *Desiring the Kingdom: Worship, Worldview, and Cultural Formation*. Grand Rapids: Baker, p. 133.

... human knowing of God is mediated through formation, imitation, affectivity, intuition, imagination, interiorization, and symbolic engagement. Thus, rather than propositions constituting the best form of catechesis, perhaps images, metaphors, paradoxes, humor, ritual, and stories mediated by a diversity of approaches – such as music, artistic media and modelling – may be better.[5]

Thus, if acts of devotion (Smith) and faith acquisition (Yong) are responses to what is felt and sensed, then theologies can equally emerge from these sources, fuelled by the imagination. Craig Dykstra has written about the 'pastoral imagination', which refers to a person's capacity for seeing a particular ministry situation's relational and sacred complexity and developing a response that is wise in judgement and action.[6] Building on this, Scharen and Campbell-Reed argue, 'Learning pastoral imagination can lead to greater integration of complex layers of knowing, a keen perception which sees situations as spaces of God's presence and work, and intuitive judgment regarding fitting responses required in the moment.'[7] Both link imagination to a way of seeing, in this case, 'seeing' means perceiving a situation.

I take this one step farther and argue that working with photographs can expand the possibilities for perceiving, and thus for imagining possibilities within ministry practice. Images use our analogical ability to imagine that which cannot be articulated in words. Photographs are not the only means for this, of course. Text-based metaphors are used throughout the Bible to describe spiritual truths. 'The Kingdom of heaven is like ... ' Sarah Arthur, writing about storytelling and youth ministry, argues that ' ... imagination is the image-making faculty of the intellect that helps us discover, process, and creatively express coherent meaning.'[8] Thus, I am suggesting that working creatively with photographs pro-actively engages the 'image-making faculty of the intellect' and thus opens up new possibilities for theological reflection.

Images in theological reflection

Patricia O'Connell Killen and John de Beer wrote *The Art of Theological Reflection* to equip people to incorporate emotions into their process of theological reflection.[9] A key stage in their 'movement to insight' is to invite reflectors to use an image to give

[5]Amos Yong. 2007. *Theology and Down Syndrome: Reimagining Disability in Late Modernity*. Waco: Baylor University Press, p. 208.

[6]Craig Dykstra. 2008. 'Pastoral and Ecclesial Imagination', in Dorothy C. Bass and Craig Dykstra, eds. *For Life Abundant: Practical Theology, Theological Education, and Christian Ministry*. Grand Rapids: Eerdmans, pp. 41–61.

[7]Christian Scharen and Eileen Campbell-Reed. 2016. 'Learning Pastoral Imagination: A Five-Year Report On How New Ministers Learn in Practice', *Auburn Studies*. Auburn Theological Seminary.

[8]Sarah Arthur. 2007. *The God-Hungry Imagination*. Nashville: Upper Room Books, p. 53.

[9]Patricia O'Connell Killen and John de Beer. 1999. *The Art of Theological Reflection*. New York: Cross Road.

shape to their feelings in relation to an incident. For them, an image may be visual, tactile, olfactory, aural, savoury or metaphoric language. They explain:

> The image provides a felt connection with our experience and directs a reflective attention to it in new ways. It bears the life-energy present in the feelings of the experience and so continues our affective engagement with the original event. The image also directs our attention to the meaning of the experience by separating us slightly from the immediate intensity of the feelings the experience contained.

So, we see that the image accomplishes two tasks in aiding reflection. First, it helps us to understand how we emotionally relate to the experience. In this way the image resonates with our experience and articulates it in a non-intellectual yet emotionally intelligent way. Moreover, the image also works in quite a different way to generate distance from the situation. By creating a slightly different relationship with the incident, the image gives us a view from a new angle. Thus, fresh attitudes and opportunities may rise to the surface. Through creating a new relationship to the situation, the image facilitates unexpected meaning to emerge from our experience. Furthermore, in Killen and de Beer's experience, 'images resist our effort to control them, suppress them, or predict their full meaning'.[10] They argue that this untamed nature of the image enables God's Word to speak uniquely into the experience. For them, it is this aspect of the image that is particularly helpful within the reflective moment to move beyond certitude and self-reliance into exploring new insight and meanings.

Others have also recognized the potential of using images within theological reflection. For example, Gary O'Neill adapted Killen and De Beer's approach and developed a model that places an image at the centre of conversations between theological sources, because 'the centring of the four-source model around an image encourages the imagination … '[11] Not only does the image engage the imagination, but Courtney Goto explains how using art within theological reflection enables a 'decentring' which can lead to 'an expanded notion of reflecting that gives form to the sayable and ineffable'.[12] Building on this and focusing on photographs, as mentioned in Chapter 5, Linda Hopkins and Eleanor Wort observed that using photographs enables more than an articulation of faith, it opens up the possibilities for 'dis-articulation', meaning that people are able to use images when words are not adequate.[13]

---

[10]Ibid., p. 38.

[11]Gary O'Neill and Liz Shercliff. 2018. *Straw for the Bricks: Theological Reflection in Practice*. London: SCM, p. 169.

[12]Courtney Goto. 2016. 'Reflecting Theologically by Creating Art: Giving Form to More than We Can Say', *Reflective Practice: Formation and Supervision in Ministry* 36: 80.

[13]Linda Hopkins and Eleanor Wort. 2020. 'Photo Elicitation and Photovoice: How Visual Research Enables Empowerment, Articulation, and Dis-Articulation', *Ecclesial Practices* 7: 163–86.

Much has been written elsewhere about the power of the visual to communicate and engage with theology, and I hope that this book contributes to considering how photographs are a particularly generative medium for doing this. For the remainder of this chapter, I will focus on examples of how photographs resource theological reflection. We will see in the examples below evidence of photographs opening spaces for connecting experience with emotions.

Doing theological reflection with photographs

Creating spaces for deeper reflection

I used photographs as part of a small research project, 'Exploring the reflective practice of Anglican laity'[14] to discover how people theologically reflect before they know that is what they are doing. Working with two other researchers, we asked participants to share a significant life event, and then describe to us how they 'processed the event' or 'worked it through'. One woman explained how she took a photograph of a winter flowering bush encountered on a walk and used this picture to help her make sense of her significant event. 'But through this little bush, it just brought back a sense of, I haven't been abandoned. I might not understand it all but that was okay in that actually God hadn't left and it was all still there, I just needed to open myself back up to it.' It became evident that she expected God to speak through nature – a form of *terra divina*. And then, to aid this reflection, she carried this image with her on her phone to remind her that life is constantly changing.

> 'There's movement, you can see a flower one day and then you look at it again another day and it's changed, and opening up, so there's a transformation from when it's a bud to when it's fully formed. I suppose at that time, that's how I would see it if I was writing something down or was thinking of something that I thought God was telling me. I think of it as, you sit with it and watch it become something.'

She returned to the bush and photographed it multiple times over the next few months, watching it change. Taking the photographs became a form of attentiveness to nature and God's way of working in the world. Gazing at the photographs on her phone reminded her of God's active presence in her life. We also see from her comments that taking photographs was seen as equivalent to writing and thinking about God's work in her life.

---

[14]Sarah Dunlop, Catherine Nancekievill, and Pippa Ross-McCabe. 2021. 'Exploring the Reflective Practice of Anglican Laity: Finding Manna in the Desert', *Practical Theology* 14 (4): 309–22. https://www.tandfonline.com/doi/full/10.1080/1756073X.2021.1957074

In addition, as part of the project, we asked people to choose a photo from an archive[15] that encapsulated their 'processing' of the significant event. In a sense, we were inviting them to continue theologically reflecting on the event, while we watched and listened to them explain their choice of image. One person chose an image that is mostly blurred but contains one point that is in focus. Until this point, he had described his experience in quite rational terms, but with the photograph he was able to explain how the emotions of the difficult situation affected his prayers. Another person chose a photograph of a baby bird held in a human hand to illustrate his processing of an unexpected change of plans. Through looking at the photograph, he came to relate the bird's vulnerability with his own and discover how his own sense of vulnerability was also held within the safety of God's care for him. We observed that using photographs in this way opened spaces to talk about the intuited, imagined and felt nature of the process of relating life events to faith. The photographs helped people to 'see' aspects of their situation that had previously been unclear to them. The photographs enabled participants to delve deeper into the situation beyond a rational explanation and to access some of the emotional responses that they experienced.

Building faith in self and others

Pavlína Kašparová has developed a process for theological reflection as an aspect of her PhD work to develop a theory of art as a living theology. For four years she photographed abandoned gloves.[16] She created posters and a video as part of an imaginary campaign, 'Glove ~~Migration~~ Adoption'.[17] Returning to this subject repeatedly for her photographs led to reflections about

> ' … the reality of consumerism which does not seek a long lifetime for "useful" products and promotes overproduction as a norm. However, such an approach can, in its most extreme form, ratify the devaluation of human beings when they lose their "usefulness" as well.'[18]

For her, the lost gloves came to represent vulnerable people on the streets, facing dehumanization and exclusion from society. This reflection awakened in her questions about how it feels to be lost, without a home and voice, even to be nearly invisible. For her, working with visual material operated like a journal through which she practiced

---

[15]We used a set of fifty numbered photographs produced by Soularium, mentioned in the previous chapter. https://www.cru.org/us/en/train-and-grow/share-the-gospel/outreach-strategies/soularium.html [accessed 8 July 2021].

[16]The artwork was displayed at an online collective exhibition *Sustainability Art Prize* at The School of Art (ARU) curated by Marina Velez in May 2020. https://www.sustainabilityartprize.com/pavlina-kasparova

[17]https://www.youtube.com/watch?v=r0MdwnjGf0c

[18]Pavlína Kašparová. 2022. 'Art as a Living Theology: Exploring Artists' Vocation', PhD Thesis for Anglia Ruskin University, p. 105.

theological reflection. The photographs enabled her to spot cultural norms that were questioned when brought into critical conversation with her Christian theology. She used the photographs to create posters designed to subvert and question societal assumptions about the disposability and dirtiness of those who live on the street (Figure 8.1). The project linked to her own sense of displacement as a foreigner living abroad, but also led to developing theologies of human worth and dignity. Even more significantly, wrestling with these themes enabled her to interrogate her own emotional reactions. Faced with guilty feelings about her own preconceptions about homeless people, continuing to photograph the lost gloves created a space to sit with her emotions. She came to see that she needed to practice self-compassion in order to have the capacity to show compassion to others. In this way, the practice of photographing along a theme became a formative process, which helped her to separate her emotions from her actions and decisions.

For Kašparová, this growth begins with personal identity construction, then moves towards buttressing the Church community, and then works itself out into creating bridges with wider culture. She observed that when facilitating theological reflection projects with other people, they are free to choose their own level of engagement, because sitting with emotional reactions may feel uncomfortable. This then creates the space to get to the heart of a matter and may help to establish faith in new forms. Kašparová argues that visual language helps people to reach new levels of understanding and creates opportunities to pause with a photograph that has touched a chord in one's heart.

Figure 8.1 Card n. 5: 'Glove ~~Migration~~ Adoption'. Created by Pavlína Kašparová. Used with permission.

Attending over scrolling

As part of her PhD research, Sal Bateman has pioneered a method of using landscape photography for theological reflection. She sets up the activity with these words: 'Photography is an immersive practice, a lived, embodied experience. You may have something on your mind, a question, an unresolved tension, a pastoral concern, or have no agenda. Take your camera and start exploring.'[19] In addition, she draws upon photographic principles for guiding the reflection, which she summarizes with the acronym 'REFLECT'. This refers to Rules within photography, such as thirds, odds and simplicity. Expert refers to considering one's own stance within the photograph. Framing and Light are also to be given careful attention. Essence of the subject is about placement, viewpoint, focus, symmetry, etc. And finally, the Colour palette and Timing (movement, etc) are elements that are considered in the crafting and analysis of the photographs. REFLECT functions as an aide memoire for considering the variety of components within a photograph, not an exhaustive list that needs to be followed. Later, after some time or movement has created distance from the process of taking the photographs, participants are invited to theologically reflect, using the images that they created. These questions may be used as helpful prompts:

- What do you notice first in your image? Has this changed?
- Anything you notice now that you didn't see before? How does this change the image? Any unintended consequences in the creation of your image?
- Is the image's narrative harmonious or are there unresolved tensions?
- What (if anything) is hidden in plain sight?
- What is missing from the image?
- What different insights (if any) did you notice from the embodied reflection compared with using REFLECT analogously away from the site of creation?
- Where was God in the process? Any scripture passages come to mind?

After this private reflection, participants are invited to share with a reflective partner, and consider:

- Is the narrative you set out to tell the one you created in the image?
- Any differences to the one you shared with your reflective partner? Why?
- How does the image narrative shared compare with your partner's interpretation (using REFLECT)? What are the key similarities or differences?
- How does your interpretation of REFLECT resonate with Scripture, tradition, reason and experience?
- What Scriptural texts resonate with the image(s) and narrative?

---

[19]Sal Bateman. 2023. *23-01-24 Handout.pdf*, PhD research for ARU.

Bateman's initial impressions are that because this approach includes an individual reflection as well as collective experience, this ensures individuals engage in theological reflection in the present, even if considering events from the past. Indeed, working as a group or in pairs adds different insights to the reflective process. Furthermore, the REFLECT process is counter-cultural because it encourages participants to take time for attentiveness to an image and theological reflection, rather than quickly scrolling through pictures embedded within social media. What I think is interesting about this approach is that it is not just the embodied act of taking photographs that adds to the insights gained, but Bateman has included the very fundamentals of photographic compositions as conversation partners in the theological reflection. She argues that the open-ended methodology of REFLECT may initially seem overwhelming, but she has found that it gives participants agency in choice of focus where other approaches may appear restrictive.

Untamed photos compelling one into new territory

Another example is found in a photography project that Ruth Barry did as a theological reflection while training for ministry. She was serving on placement within a group of small rural parishes on the outskirts of a large city. There she encountered the challenging issue of families bypassing the small village church in favour of travelling into the larger, well-resourced churches in the city centre. She recounts:

> One day during morning prayer on my placement, as I was sitting in the stillness of one of the beautiful churches in the shaft of sunlight that came through the windows, I was reflecting on these parishes and all the various events I had experienced, and I received the picture of an alpine plant with tiny beautiful white flowers. Small, yet lovely and flourishing in its environment. As I contemplated this image it was followed by the image of an enormous rhododendron bush, covered in vibrant pompoms of flowers, stunning in its beauty. These two images were seared in my brain and I knew they were speaking to my understanding of what "success" looks like in churches.

After this incident, she found that she began to notice tiny, unobtrusive flowers in all sorts of unlikely places. She began taking photographs to record her observations and reflections. She found that her focus shifted from sized-based measurements of success towards noticing flourishing. She produced a series of six photographs which began with a close-up of a crocus, then gradually zoomed out to show a sea of small blooms at the base of large trees. She submitted these as the creative component of an assessed theological reflection, and they formed part of an end of term exhibition (see Figure 8.2, below).

Figure 8.2 Series of photographs by Ruth Barry. Used with permission.

What we see here is that in a moment of prayer, she had a sense of her own mind processing a situation and, guided by the spirit of God, she visualized the flowers. This image then causes her to become more attentive to spotting small flowers. This new way of seeing, inspired by God, led to further reflection as she started to record her observations through taking photographs. Her focus was shifted from success to flourishing, which created new meanings and possibilities within her ministry. She wrote:

> I had a sudden insight into the verse 1 Corinthians 3:9 that the church is God's field. Paul was using the analogy to explain that it was ultimately the power of God that caused plants to increase and grow, no significance should be attached to the workers who plant or water other than the part they play in seeing God's field flourish, ultimately it is God who has caused the increase (1Cor 3:7). And most importantly the Church is *God's* field, all of it, all the plants and all the workers.

In this way, Scripture and the photographs worked together to enable her to develop a nuanced and complexified theology concerning how God is at work in different contexts.

What I love about this is that as she took the close-up pictures, she became aware of the wider view, causing her to widen the frame to the larger picture. This simulates a helpful process within ministry too, of looking beyond the immediate to the bigger picture. By creating a series of images, she was able to convey this transition visually. In fact, the series can also be read in reverse – moving from the wide view and zooming in to a close up of one flower. Looking back on this, she reflected that sometimes she still needs to remember to pay attention to the seemingly small, insignificant moments of ministry. At other times it's important to be reminded of the bigger picture. Embracing this tension and intentionally pivoting between perspectives has hugely resourced her own spirituality as she has moved into church leadership.

Another layer of this reflective process is that photographs may have an enduring place within everyday life, unlike other forms of theology. The photographs that Ruth produced are visually stimulating and aesthetically pleasing. In her first clergy job after training, she placed the printed series of photographs on the wall of her study. She joked that one wouldn't frame an essay from training college and put it on the wall, but this series of photographs worked perfectly there. She recounted that the pictures reminded her that both perspectives are needed in ministry – attention to the short, one-to-one interactions with an individual and the larger events with hundreds of people. In this way, insights from her years of training were translated into material objects that became aid memoirs within her current ministry, continuing to resource her practice. Because of the medium, this visual theology then took on new meanings in later chapters of ministry.

We see here a cycle of photographic theological reflection based on her experience. An image was given by God, which is processed by that person, who then worked with it through the lens of a camera and produced images that conveyed new theological insights. The printed photographs displayed within everyday workspace facilitated further theological reflection when new situations were encountered. This is a form of visual theology in process.

Conclusion

Visual ways of knowing bypass purely cognitive frameworks and lead to creative theologies which make sense of tradition, scripture and lived experience. This is why imagination is central to theological reflection. In this chapter, I've argued that photographs are a highly generative approach to doing theological reflection. They help to engage the image-making component of the theological imagination. Using an archive of photographs can ignite the imagination because as we gaze at the images, we imagine seeing the scene portrayed and we wonder what else is happening beyond the frame. We become curious about the gaze of the photographer and why they are drawing our attention to this scene. In this way, the photographs invite us to see possibilities and to be curious about what is unknown or not yet experienced. Photographs open up new spaces for reflecting on life and ministry through the eyes of faith.

In my own study of how people theologically reflect before they realize that is what they are doing, we saw that the photographs created a unique distance from the situation which opened up space for viewing the experience from a new angle. When Kašparová spent years photographing stray gloves, she gained a whole new appreciation of the vulnerability of being lost, which developed her own faith and enabled her to build the faith others both inside and outsider her faith community.

Bateman found that intentional engagement with photographs caused people to pause their habitual infinite scroll of images and instead to linger in groups over photographs, leading to new insights. Barry discovered that not only the process of taking photographs, but also their production and use led to new reflections to resource her ministry. Photographs worked as stimuli for reflections and the taking and viewing of photographs enabled attentiveness, which led to opportunities for new insights and deeper, prayerful reflections.

At the start of this chapter, I defined theological reflection as a spiritually sensitive and attentive process of making sense of life in light of faith. Life experiences may be positive or may linger in our memories because they are quite difficult. Hedy Bach, mentioned in Chapter 5, argues that 'photographs can help us to acknowledge what has previously been resisted and repressed, so that we may let go, reflect and grow from our experiences'.[20] Telling stories about our photographs can help to 'unfreeze memories'. For her, 'photograph' is not merely a noun to describe a product or print but is an active verb for learning. 'Photographs slow time into moments, moments that can be studied.' In this way, photographs become 'transitional objects toward another reality', like stepping-stones towards meaning and narrative truth. This leads us to the subject of the next chapter, how photographs can resource spirituality.

---

[20]Hedy Bach. 2001. 'The Place of the Photograph in Visual Narrative Research', *Afterimage* 29 (3): 7. https://online.ucpress.edu/afterimage/article-abstract/29/3/7/191563/The-Place-of-the-Photograph-in-Visual-Narrative?redirectedFrom=fulltext

9

Photographs and Spirituality: Seeing and Being Seen

One of my creative outlets is working with stained glass pieces edged in copper foil. I love how the colours of this art form shift as the light shining through it changes throughout the day. During a stained-glass retreat, I managed to craft a piece inspired by Rublev's Trinity icon. I had spent the past year drawing my ideas, discarding them and drawing again. I had first become interested in icons when I was researching Ukrainian young people's spirituality for my PhD. I read widely about icons but was particularly inspired by Henri Nouwen's commentary on the Trinity icon, which expanded and complexified my theology of the Trinity.[1] I was drawn to the possibility of spiritual formation that happens whilst gazing at an icon. On a trip to Moscow, I was able to visit Tretyakov Gallery Arts Museum and view Rublev's famous work, which only deepened my desire to incorporate visual forms into my own devotional practice. Like a good tourist, I bought a much smaller replica icon to take home.

Years later, during the strange years of the pandemic, I joined many others in taking up a lockdown hobby. My mother had taught me the basics of foil-wrapped stained glass when I was a teenager, and I slowly re-learned the skills necessary, gradually buying the tools I needed. Making an icon out of glass was my own way of expressing how hospitality and relationship are built deeply into God's own nature. In choosing the colours of glass, I followed traditional colour canons for icons: Jesus is wearing a red tunic with blue robe, to symbolize his humanity clothed with the divine. The Holy Spirit is green for new life. And the Father is gold for the one who dwells in the divine realm. The icon is framed in gold, to portray that the godhead exists in heaven. The design contained a lot of curves, particularly around the bevelled roundels which were used for the heads and halos. Cutting glass to fit around these can be problematic, particularly for an amateur like me, because curves are very difficult to cut into glass without it breaking in the wrong place. I decided that there is 'grace in the space' and

---

[1]Henri Nouwen. 1987. *Behold the Beauty of the Lord: Praying with Icons*. Notre Dame: Ave Maria Press.

Figure 9.1 'Trinity Icon in Stained Glass'. Photograph by Sarah Dunlop.

left the centre of the icon open around the three heads. Once the piece was finished, I was cautiously pleased with the result, and I hung it in my window.

However, when I went to photograph the icon to share with others, I ran into difficulty, because the empty spaces meant that shapes of houses and trees beyond the window could be seen in the background. It was hard to find the right angle for the camera to capture the light coming through the glass, without the distraction of the objects in the background. The camera's lens flattened what was visible, equating the background with the glass. But this wrestling with the camera led me to a new discovery. As I moved the piece around, I was seeing the world through the Trinity. Unlike Rublev's icon, which is made of wood, my icon actually created a way of seeing through, via, the Divine. The camera had given me a new way of seeing something that I thought I had already seen. And this led me to new levels of contemplation – pushing me from an inward appreciation of the hospitality of God towards an outward movement of considering the divine gracious presence in the world, and my place in this new perspective.

In the previous two chapters, I have made the case that in ministry, photographs can create spaces for encounter between people and between people and their contexts. I then discussed how photographs can ignite the imagination, taking theological reflection in new directions and opening up the possibilities for deepening and expanding theology. This final chapter builds on and includes these ways that photographs can resource theology, but here the focus is on spirituality. I will make the case that using photographs helps us not only to see our world in new ways but gives us fresh perspectives on how God sees the world. Even more importantly, I will argue that photography may enable a deep sense of *being* seen by the living God. Photographs accompany us on the inward journey and propel us outward into witness.

In Chapter 2, I mentioned Terence Heng's guide to creating photographs for qualitative social scientific research. In the introduction, he observed that one aspect of the power of using photographs is that they work to 'provoke desire', meaning that they point to meanings beyond a surface reading.[2] In this chapter, I am taking this idea further and arguing that photographs may 'provoke' a desire for God. Rosalind Pearmain wrote that 'Spirituality is about deeply stirring and moving experiences'.[3] In the Introduction, I referred to Pearmain's observations regarding the importance of visual material as evocative cues to resource research about spirituality. Although this chapter is about personal spirituality, not studies of spirituality, her principles remain central to what I call 'affective knowing'. She observes that when we access this knowledge via visual material, we open up a bigger space in which to find resonance with spiritual experiences. Working with photographs embraces this affective knowing about God and widens the possibilities for contemplation. First, I will give three examples of how photographs can enhance spiritual practices: spiritual life maps, practicing presence and *visio divina*. In the second part of the chapter, I will explore issues around 'the gaze', how ways of seeing can deepen spiritual practices.

Documenting the spiritual life

Creating a spiritual life map is an activity developed for use within spiritual direction and other forms of pastoral care. Its use was inspired by Augustine's *Confessions* and

---

[2]Heng argues that photographs used for research purposes should have three functions, to inform, to represent and to provoke desire. Terence Heng. 2016. *Visual Methods in the Field: Photography for the Social Sciences*. Abingdon: Routledge, p. 6.

[3]Rosalind Pearmain. 2007. 'Evocative Cues and Presence: Relational Consciousness within Qualitative Research', *International Journal of Children's Spirituality* 12 (1): 75–82, p. 79.

is a visual means of representing the narrative of a person's spiritual pilgrimage and associated events. It pictures a person's relationship with God over time, forming a map of a person's spiritual life.[4] When using a life map as a spiritual exercise, one might draw a path or timeline, adding in significant life events and points of conversion and any other key turning points that have spiritual significance. This is a valuable exercise, because it may help a person to identify how God has acted in their life and to spot any patterns of behaviour. It can give people a fresh perspective on their spiritual journey.

With the preponderance of people using photographs to document their life on social media, this cultural practice can be harnessed for reflection. Rather than merely trying to recall past events, a person could look through their own social media posts or their camera feed on their smartphone. Gazing at these glimpses of the past may help to remind a person about not just what happened, but their feelings about it at the time, thus accessing their affective knowing. The pictures may do a better job than words of conveying the heart of the matter within situations. However, just as our memories can distort the past, so a photograph should not be seen as a definitive representation of the true situation. When using a photo feed as a means of telling the story of one's life, it is worth pondering what motivates us to lift the camera and take the photograph. What are we documenting? Are we including both high points and low points? And, if we are looking at a social media feed, one must consider the accuracy of the story that one is telling about oneself to the wider public. Thus, using photographs as an aide-memoire for a life map should be done judiciously, keeping in mind what events are missing from the feed.

Another documentary style approach is to intentionally take photographs to explore a spiritual journey. For example, working with a photographer, Thomas Quartier used a series of staged photographs of himself over a three-year period to visually portray his transition from his professional career as a scholar in a university to being a monk in a monastery who works as a scholar. These photographs were published within the three books that he wrote to chart this spiritual transition. For him, these photographs do much more than illustrate his writing, they have a spiritual function, inviting the viewer to consider their own spiritual transformation. For him, this introspection then becomes an outward movement of invitation into the spiritual life.[5]

---

[4]See David Hodge. 2005. 'Spiritual Lifemaps: A Client-Centered Pictorial Instrument for Spiritual Assessment, Planning, and Intervention', *Social Work* 50 (1): 77–87. https://www.researchgate.net/publication/8043219_Spiritual_Lifemaps_A_Client-Centered_Pictorial_Instrument_for_Spiritual_Assessment_Planning_and_Intervention [accessed 21 July 2023].
[5]Thomas Quartier. 2019. 'Shooting Monastic Identity: Reflections on Photography and Spiritual Transformation', in Marcin Jewdokimow and Thomas Quartier, eds. *A Visual Approach to the Study of Religious Orders*. Abingdon: Routledge, pp. 79–105.

Practicing presence

Our contemporary society teaches us to read images quickly – too quickly – we process and assess them in milliseconds. We need to do this to survive in our visually stimulating environment. But engaging in spiritual practices is often about slowing down, pausing, seeing, noticing – essentially being in the moment. Certainly, this is a key component of the mindfulness movement. It is also a core element of contemplative forms of spirituality. In this section, I explore the work of a number of people who demonstrate how photography can help develop spiritual ways of practicing presence; attending to the present moment.

Philip Richter, whose work using photographs within research was mentioned in Chapter 2, has also explored how taking photographs can become a spiritual activity. This approach is outlined *Spirituality in Photography*, a practical book with exercises, space to write reflections and tips about using equipment, including smartphone cameras. He outlines different photographic principles such as framing, perspective and telling a story and relates these skills to aspects of spirituality. He explains that photography as a spirituality requires slowing down and noticing. He recommends stopping and just using one's eyes to carefully see and notice details. Ask 'Where is my attention drawn? Where is the energy in the scene? What is majestic?' He even suggests that another way of seeing before even taking a photo is to draw what is of interest. It does not need to be a skilful drawing, but the act helps one to really spend time noticing and looking. He believes that carefully crafted photographs 'have the capacity to deepen our vision and sharpen our sense of what life is all about'.[6] Referring to the work of Valerie Isenhower, he notes that just as a photographer may edit their photographs after a shoot, so reviewing one's photographs at the end of the day can be a form of prayer, asking 'What did I learn about myself today?' And 'How has today helped me grow closer to God?'[7] His work demonstrates that photography and spirituality are generative for each other.[8]

Along similar lines to Richter's 'slowing down and noticing', former Royal Air Force chaplain Stephen Radley discovered the practice of photography enabled him to live in the 'now', a practice which was life-giving after experiencing post-traumatic stress. After retiring from the RAF, he undertook a diploma in professional photography. He said in an interview, 'While studying for the diploma,

---

[6]Philip Richter. 2017. *Spirituality in Photography: Taking Pictures with Deeper Vision*. London: Darton, Longman and Todd, p. 9.

[7]Ibid., p. 100, referring to Valerie K. Isenhower. 2012. *Meditation on Both Sides of the Camera: A Spiritual Journey in Photography*. Nashville: Upper Room Books.

[8]Along similar lines, but with more information about elements of composition including using natural light, see: David Tinney and Denise McGuiness. 2020. *Available Light: Awakening Spirituality through Photography*. Pittsburgh, PA: Dorrance Publishing. The book includes the author's own photographs and ideas for reflection.

I realised how it was much about composition and how we see life, rather than the technical aspects … I realised photography was very mindful. Indeed, I found that the whole practice of going out and taking pictures was quite therapeutic, helping to calm anxious thoughts.'[9] The practice of contemplative photography helped him to gain a new appreciation for life and provided emotional space to focus on helping others. He now facilitates contemplative photography workshops and retreats because he believes that this practice can promote mental and emotional health for many people. This entails spending time looking at photographs. For example, within his workshops, he encourages people to 'listen to an image', which entails noticing what is going on inside them emotionally as they look at an image. He believes that this listening to the self enables one to connect these emotions to other areas of life. Contemplative photography also involves taking photographs. He suggests that people can adapt their everyday photography from: [*that's nice, snap*] to: [*that's nice –* **PAUSE** *– focus and create a picture*]. He writes, 'The pause centres us in the present moment which can help us find peace of mind, develop relationships and strengthen our resilience leading to greater happiness and contentment.'[10] He also frames this theologically, arguing that photography helps to move him to a *kairos* moment. This pause creates a space for hearing from God. 'We can meet God only in the present (lacking a time machine, we cannot meet God in the past or the future), and photography reveals God in the detail of life and all its wonder.'[11]

Stephen Radley co-authored a book *Letting Photos Speak* with Philip Richter and Andy Lindley. Their book explains a contemplative approach to taking photos, what they refer to as the practice of 'mindful photography'. They describe how this works in practice in the Introduction:

> Within mindful photography we leave our camera in its bag or our pocket until we feel a connection with wherever we are. That connection arises by noticing and becoming aware of our physical surroundings and our emotions, and, once that happens, the wonder of the present opens before us. Mindful photography is open to mystery and surprise, never knowing what each moment will hold. It is a genre of photography which is free from judgement – the idea that a picture can be good or bad – and filled with wonder and revelation.[12]

---

[9]The interview was part of the publicity following winning the Amateur Photographer Unsung Hero Award in 2021. https://www.amateurphotographer.co.uk/apawards/ap-awards-2021-our-unsung-hero-145779 [accessed 18 July 2023]. Radley has been influenced by Howard Zehr's 2005 book, *Little Book of Contemplative Photography: Seeing With Wonder, Respect and Humility*. Good Books, Intercourse, PA.

[10]https://soulfulvision.uk/approach/ [accessed 18 July 2023].

[11]https://www.churchtimes.co.uk/articles/2021/4-june/features/features/photography-therapeutic-work-of-sights-and-insights [accessed 18 July 2023].

[12]Stephen Radley, Philip Richter and Andy Lindley. 2023. *Letting Photos Speak: Visio Divina and Other Approaches to Contemplative Photography*. London: Darton, Longman and Todd, p. 17.

They observe that having a camera on the smart phone in the pocket means that the power of using photography to support one's well-being is available at any moment. This practice serves to anchor people to their current physical environment and emotional state.

Praying with the eyes

Lectio divina, divine reading, is a spiritual practice that entails reading, meditating, praying and contemplating scriptural texts. Mark Oestreicher, whose work I referred to in Chapter 7, recommends that his archive of black-and-white photos can support the process of *lectio divina*. He observes, 'The aim of *Lectio Divina* is not to study or gain information, but to listen with the heart to the whispers of the Spirit.'[13] He suggests that a person could read a passage of scripture three times, pausing between readings. After the third reading, they can reflect and meditate on the passage. Then they can choose a photo from the archive that connects with what God might be saying and journal any revelations. Additionally, he notes that another form of *lectio divina* is to read a narrative passage of Scripture several times and imagine oneself as one of the characters within it. After doing this and processing what has been experienced through this imagining, a photograph can be chosen that connects with the thoughts that emerged from the reading.

Visio divina is 'divine seeing' and replaces the reading of *lectio* with looking. It is a spiritual practice, a way of praying with one's eyes, that expands one's ability to see the world through the eyes of God. This has some resonance with the ritual use of icons within the Orthodox tradition. Icons follow an established theological cannon and are visual forms of theology. They are also designed to draw the viewer into the heavenly realm.[14] However, *visio divina* is bigger than contemplating icons and is not even limited to sacred art. Instead, all visual forms are potential avenues for seeing something of God's presence in the world. *Visio divina* can be a way of noticing and embracing wonder. This very act can function as a form of prayer because the revelation of God evokes a response from the viewer, leading to a kind of dialogue with God. Space is created for listening and being transformed by this divine encounter.

Elizabeth Manneh has recently written a five-step process for doing *visio divina*. She first starts with a prayer and then prayerfully chooses a photograph to use. She notes that sometimes it is helpful to put the image in the centre of a scrapbook page,

---

[13]Mark Oestreicher. 2013. *Every Picture Tells a Story: 48 Evocative Photographs for Inspiring Reaction and Reflection*. The Youth Cartel, LLC, p. 41. www.theyouthcartel.com

[14]Stephen Binz has combined *lectio* and *visio divina* into one practice, using Scripture and icons. His method is outlined in his 2016 book, *Discovering the Power of Lectio and Visio Divina*. Notre Dame: Ave Maria Press.

so that as she works through the steps, she can make notes and drawings around the photo. Third, she allows her eyes to be drawn to something within the image, and focuses on that, slowing her breathing and paying attention to her thoughts and emotions. Fourth, she zooms out and gazes at the image as a whole, looking at anything else that catches her eye. In this phase, she not only is paying attention to her thoughts and feelings but considering whether these direct her to a passage of Scripture. Fifth, she spends time in silence, considering whether any message from God is emerging. Sixth, she responds through journaling and praying about the experience. Sometimes she places the page in a visible place that will remind her of what has emerged. She reflects that for her, *visio divina* has opened up new forms of communication with God.[15]

Stephen Obold Eshleman is a healthcare chaplain and amateur photographer who finds that creating art through photography enables him to contemplate and express aspects of his existence that he cannot find words to describe. He also writes of how the practice of photography enables him to slow down, be present in the moment and to notice details. 'There are moments when I feel connected to something much greater, much larger than myself. These moments are ineffable, conveying meaning beyond words.'[16] He has discovered that the movement inward has turned outward – the photographs that helped him to regain his sense of self in the midst of his demanding work now support others. He observes that just as spiritual care in a healthcare facility needs to transcend religious creed and relate to feelings such as hope, joy and fear, so photographs offer a language to carry these emotions and provide a means for spiritual exploration. He has begun to bring a small number of his landscape photographs onto a ward and invites a person to choose which one most reflects his or her life now. In this way, he argues that the photograph becomes a third voice in the conversation, mediating between the chaplain and the patient. Thus, the photograph becomes the one inviting a person to reflect upon their life. Eshleman observes that this enables a person to enter into the space between one's outer and inner worlds and see where they converge. This involves not looking, as though trying to find something preconceived within the photograph, but seeing, being open and receptive to what the photograph may offer. Eshleman's differentiation between looking and seeing is helpful as, in the following section, I turn to consider the nature of the 'gaze' within spirituality.

---

[15]Elizabeth Manneh. 2023. 'Praying with Your Eyes: How to Get Started with Visio Divina', a Ministry Resource article on the Roman Catholic Paulist Fathers website *Busted Halo*. https://bustedhalo.com/ministry-resources/praying-with-your-eyes-how-to-get-started-with-visio-divina [accessed 19 July 2023].

[16]Stephen F. Obold Eshleman and Shelley E. Varner Perez. 2022. '"I Don't Do Religion": Using Nature Photographs to Engage Patients in Spiritual Reflection', *Journal of Pain and Symptom Management* 64 (5): e305–e309, https://doi.org/10.1016/j.jpainsymman.2021.07.034.

The gaze

It seems to me, that when employing photographs in the service of spirituality, the nature of the gaze is of utmost importance. American philosopher Susan Sontag offered a wide-ranging critique of photography, particularly as an infallible means of knowing. For her, the photographer's gaze was voyeuristic and taking a picture was an act of aggression. She sees the worst of human failings as exemplified in the act of taking photographs. She famously wrote, 'to photograph people is to violate them … it turns people into objects that can be symbolically possessed.'[17] Her concerns are worth noting, in the sense that the photographer's character matters. The intention behind the act of pressing the shutter button (or the digital capture button) is hugely significant. Rather than *being* in a moment, if I am trying to *capture* the moment on camera there is a very real danger of missing the moment. Thus, the camera prevents me from being present and, as Sontag warns, can actually create a distance between myself and my situation. Some members of the royal family have said that they dislike camera phones, because when they go out to meet people, they are met with a sea of camera phones, rather than people's faces engaging them in eye contact.[18] Perhaps an aspect of the spirituality of photography is sensing when to put the camera away, and to just see, taste and experience the now.

Thomas Merton, the spiritual writer and Trappist monk, discovered photography whilst he lived in solitude in his hermitage. His camera became a tool for meditation and his meditations were enriched by his photographs. Richter observed that Merton's approach to photography demonstrated the 'contemplative gaze', which avoids the predatory and objective way of seeing that Susan Sontag feared accompanied photography.[19] Merton did not photograph objects to possess them, but to acknowledge their presence and connection to the immediate world. Esther de Waal, who published a collection of Merton's contemplative writings and photographs, wrote in an introductory section, 'he respected the power of God's creation to bear witness for itself. He went out to each thing, allowed it to communicate its essence, to say what it would, reveal what it would. He was always insistent on our need to "see directly what is in front of us".'[20] Here we see that the practice of photography functioned as a means of growing in deeper awareness of the 'hidden wholeness' of elements of the created world.[21] Not only was Merton committed to developing his

---

[17]Susan Sontag. 1979. *On Photography*, Penguin: Harmondsworth, p. 14.

[18]See this BBC article from 2 September 2014: https://www.bbc.co.uk/news/newsbeat-29026866 [accessed 25 July 2023].

[19]Philip Richter. 2006. 'Late Developer: Thomas Merton's Discovery of Photography as a Medium for His Contemplative Vision', *Spiritus: A Journal of Christian Spirituality* 6 (2): 195–212. https://doi.org/10.1353/scs.2006.0071

[20]Esther de Waal. 1992. *A Seven Day Journey with Thomas Merton*. Guildford, Surrey: Eagle, p. 35.

[21]John Howard Griffin. 1979. *A Hidden Wholeness: The Visual World of Thomas Merton*. Boston: Houghton, Mifflin, p. 4.

own contemplative gaze through photography, his hope was that when others looked at his photographs, their gaze too would draw them into a contemplative space.

Dominic White has explored the Christian gaze in a book called, *How Do I Look?*[22] He considered both the act of looking and the experience of being looked at by another person. Although he charts a gentle awareness of the dangers to people's spiritual and emotional well-being through the prevalence of sharing selfies (photographs taken of oneself by oneself) via social media, his book is largely hopeful. A faith-filled gaze is made possible by the spirit of Jesus Christ who redeems the brokenness of the human gaze. White argues that in a similar way, a photograph may be redeemed. 'By freezing the moment, it gives us back time to see what we did not have time to see back then, but more, it becomes a sign of the Resurrection in which death will be no more.'[23] He argues that the photograph opens up a space for gazing deeply and learning to see as God sees. The eyes of faith look for the gift in what is seen, because it is the gaze of love. He calls for a process of humbling oneself before objects and people in order to truly see them.

White turns to the tradition of praying with icons, noting that here the gaze can be turned around, and the viewer gains a sense of being seen by the divine. Indeed, this experience was transformative for me during my fieldwork in Orthodox churches among Ukrainian young people. As I prayed in cold stone churches, Christ, Mary and the saints gazed at me from the icons, inviting eye contact. Praying was done with the eyes and mouth. I discovered that this visual form of prayer was not just about seeing the holy other, but for me became a deeply spiritual experience of being seen by God. There was a mutuality in the 'seeing' – a seeing and being seen. White observes that this step is necessary for redeeming the gaze. 'I realized that to see, we need to know first, to have experienced, being seen by God, by his gaze. We cannot give what we have not got.'[24]

Before training for Anglican ministry, Mark Tatton was a professional portrait photographer who had come to see that taking a photograph of someone was a compelling way to know them better. He was also aware that the photographer's gaze shapes how the subject is depicted, which is a vulnerable position for the person portrayed. During his training for ordained ministry, he decided to shift the balance of power by putting his camera into the hands of friends and strangers. He asked them to photograph him, and then, after they had taken time to compose and take the picture, he then asked them to write what they saw in him. Of the many photographs and interactions that he collected, he created a collage of forty-five portraits and comments. He called the project 'Iamwhoyousaylam'.

---

[22]Dominic White. 2020. *How Do I Look? Theology in the Age of the Selfie*. London: SCM.
[23]Ibid., p. 85.
[24]Ibid., p. 123.

Iamwhoyousaylam

Figure 9.2 'Iamwhoyousaylam' collage by Mark Tatton. Used with permission.

A few years after doing this project, he observed that the initial process of taking and composing the portrait enabled people to reflect visually and conceptually before they needed to think about what words to use to describe him. For him, it was a fascinating and creative way to theologically reflect on identity. One of the biggest surprises was how perfect strangers observed interesting and insightful aspects of his personality. He also noted that doing this project was more of a spiritual act than he had imagined it would be. This emerges in the poem he wrote to accompany the tableau of portraits.

> *Knowing myself to be the object of love.*
> *Learning that I am significant.*
> *Understanding what it means to be wanted.*
> *'Self-discovery' is illusive.*
> *There is no 'real me'.*
> *All I have is the 'me' that I find in you,*
> *the strange things I learn*
> *in the places we meet.*
> *Hurt, humiliation, indignity,*
> *kindness, hope, love.*
> *Beloved.*
> *Not learning to love myself,*

there are too many doubts,
but listening for the still small voice,
a gift,
subtle, surprising, disarming, opaque.
Being attentive to the whisper of grace.
The echoes of love.
Iamwhoyousaylam.

It seems to me that through this project he is fully engaging with the vulnerability of photography. He is opening himself up to the gaze to another, to be really seen. And in the end, finds something of himself within the divine gaze.

Ian Adams, contemplative writer and college chaplain, notes that a concept within contemplative Christian spirituality is a movement towards 'returning the gaze'. It entails an awareness of the divine gaze upon us that moves into a calling to return the gaze. How does one respond to the God who gazes upon us, not in critical judgement, but in love? For Adams, the photographs that he creates are for sharing the lived story of his spiritual journey. The process, similar to others discussed in this chapter, shapes him and he hopes that it may also shape the viewer. This happens because the pictures reveal a way of seeing, which may be a gift to someone else. His most recent books of contemplative writing include photographs, which are included not to illustrate the text, but to open up the possibility of connections drawn between them.[25] In an interview, I asked him why working with photographs was so important to him. He said, 'There is a humility to photography. We are not so much creating something but stumbling upon something. A veil is lifted, and we see something in a moment.'[26]

When I asked him what advice he might give to others seeking to engage photography within their spiritual practices, he said to look for wonder and be attentive to what is nurturing and surprising. He advised that the subject does not need to be conventionally beautiful. He also said that it is helpful to spend time with other photographers' works, learning from the tradition. Then, one can find one's own voice out of that. Talking about the creative and spiritual process, he said, 'It has to work on me first, and then it might work on someone else. It's similar to the approach I take to writing sermons. We don't use something just for utility, but because it is actually shaping us.' Furthermore, it is his practice to keep returning to the same subject to see what opens up. Over the last few years, he has photographed

---

[25]See Ian Adams. 2016. *Wilderness Taunts: Revealing Your Light*. London: Hymns Ancient & Modern; 2017. *Some Small Heaven: Seeking Light in Winter*. Norwich: Canterbury Press; and 2018. *Breathing Deep: Life in the Spirit of Easter*. Norwich: Canterbury Press.
[26]From an interview with Ian Adams on 30 March 2023. For example, Ian Adams kindly allowed me to use one of his photos for the cover of my 2019 book *Megachurches and Social Engagement: Public Theology in Practice*. Leiden: Brill. Ian remarks that it shows a moment of people moving around an iconic church, not necessarily towards or from it. How we see this photograph opens new possibilities for our perceptions.

Figure 9.3 A photo from the 'Empty Pool' project. Photograph by Ian Adams. Used with permission.

a pool in a Cambridge park which was left empty during the pandemic. In an article, he recounts how something within him evoked a desire to return to it to gaze upon the beauty there, even in the cracks. Yet again, he observes that photography revealed what was hidden. 'The Empty Pool project has lent weight to my instinct that art can act as a kind of sacrament, bringing into being what it points to – transformation of individual, of community and of the world. In spending time with the empty pool I have found my internal landscape being quietly reshaped.'[27]

Conclusion

This chapter has explored how photographs may be employed to resource spirituality, through tracing life events, contemplative practicing presence, and forms of visual prayer. There are of course many more ways that spiritual seekers have discovered that photographs have deepened their spiritual practices. In the latter part of the

---

[27]Ian Adams. 2021. 'The Empty Pool: Persistent Presence', *Anvil: Journal of Theology and Mission* 37 (1): 8.

chapter, I turned to a brief consideration of the gaze, proposing that photographs can actually refine and redeem the flawed human gaze. As Ian Adams noted, taking photographs enables him to see things in a different way, to find the extraordinary in the ordinary. Indeed, he went so far as to say that there was something sacramental about the process, which creates connections with the transcendent.

How do we know whether our photos are helping us to listen to the interior presence of God or are just our own internal processing? On some levels, the answer is simple. If the fruit of spiritual engagement with photographs helps us to think and act more like Jesus, and to know God better, then this creative act is a spiritually nourishing activity. One of the longest passages in Scripture about creative work is found in the account of the building of the Tabernacle in Exodus 35. Bezalel is recounted as being 'filled with divine spirit, with skill, intelligence, and knowledge in every kind of craft, to devise artistic designs … '[28] This is the first instance in the Bible of being filled with the Spirit of God, and it comes in relation to human creating. He most likely learned his skills in Egypt, and now he is invited, via a calling from the Holy Spirit, to turn his imagination to sacred objects for worship. Thus, God fills people with his divine spirit to enable them to create. And God is known more fully through creating.

---

[28]Exodus 35.31-32, *NRSVA*.

10

Conclusion: New Horizons in Theology

This book has offered ideas and techniques for doing theology with photographs. The variety of examples has demonstrated how photographs work on different levels to reveal what might otherwise have gone unmarked. I've explored how looking at and talking about photographs energizes the theological imagination for us and for others. Creating photographs challenges us to see differently, opening new possibilities for discerning divine revelation. I hope that this book is only the beginning, a launchpad others use to set off into new territories, developing new methods and approaches.

I have made the case that photographs invite us to change what it means for us to do theology. Theology is more than listening, reading and speaking. It is seeing and being seen. This mutuality of seeing extends to how research findings are shared and communicated with others. As we create exhibitions and websites to share our photographs, others are invited to join in the interpretation of visual theology. This has the potential to generate even more theology and insights as the conversations continue beyond the conclusion of the project or ministry activity. Just as photography has the potential to expand our theology, it also should open up new possibilities for how we communicate our theology.

Working with photographs opens up new horizons for doing theology within research and ministry, creating fields of shared meaning. This paves the way for new forms for theological communication within our rapidly changing cultural contexts. Artist Makoto Fujimura is cautiously hopeful about the fruitful potential for sharing photographs via social media. He writes in his book, *Art and Faith: A Theology of Making*,

> Technology and social media can be used creatively for life-giving storytelling, but they also can have life-taking results. So the 'None' generation does its making through Instagram and iPhone technology; and the power of such a legitimate way of making has not been recognised by the church, other than when it says 'let's "use" these

impulses to communicate the gospel and make disciples of these youth'. But 'using' is a utilitarian word, and I wish to affirm those who 'make' rather than 'use'.[1]

Fujimura recognizes the power of storytelling and life-sharing that can happen through technology, particularly using the smartphone camera to take and share photographs. He notes that this way of making has not been recognized by the church. He believes that engaging with these forms with a stance of creating and discovering, rather than using and transmitting, can be hugely beneficial and generative. But he also recognizes the danger of social media. It seems to me that anyone seeking to engage people in making and sharing photographs for research or ministry should also think carefully about the potential pitfalls, particularly if social media forms are being used. In both research and ministry, it is essential that the activities we create for people are life-giving not life-taking.

Nevertheless, in this era when never before have so many people held the power to make photographs with them everywhere they go, it seems to me that it would be a step forward to acknowledge sharing photographs on social media platforms can be a legitimate form of 'making'. Not only in Fujimura's sense of making art, but also in a theological sense of meaning making. That's not to say that all quickly snapped images that are shared on social media hold supreme significance. But the seeds of deep significance may lurk there. And when visual sense-making of the world encounters the possibility of transcendence, pictures of lived theologies emerge alongside their narrations. Therefore, it is important for the church to recognize that the expression of theology via photographs becomes the theology. Theology is flowing through the world at light speed, in visual forms. This is not to say that it is a more authentic theology, because it is visual, but that it is a real *expression* of theology. We are actually seeing a vision of reality, not just reading about it, or listening to it. This *showing*, not telling, is a powerful means of communicating one's world.

I have argued that photographs generate a different kind of information from text, meaning that they broaden the possibilities for knowing. This different kind of information can be a form of theology that takes into account affective knowing. This means that the possibilities for theology are expanded to include a wide range of mixed-ability people as theological knowers. Furthermore, I have observed that photographs work to create bridges between people across a variety of divisions. Meaning is developed together as people look at photographs and relate them to their own story and God's story. Working with photographs in this way increases our reflexivity, our awareness of our own preconceptions, power and position.

But doing theology with photographs is more than harnessing affective ways of knowing in both ourselves and others. The presence of Christ is in the eye of the

---

[1] The 'none' generation is those who do not identify with a particular religion when asked on surveys. Makoto Fujimura. 2021. *Art and Faith: A Theology of Making.* New Haven, CT: Yale University Press, p. 6.

theologian researcher, granting new vision as we gaze at our world through the eyes of faith.[2] For people of faith, photographs are a powerful tool for seeing the world revealed through God's loving gaze, the 'graced perspective' mentioned by White.[3] Photographs record this gaze and capture a way of seeing. They enable us to zoom in to look at the tiny details of a situation and they also enable us to zoom out to observe the big picture movements of God. Nicolas Healy observes that viewing our context through the lens of the Christian metanarrative, what he calls the 'theo-dramatic horizon', opens up the possibility for speaking prophetically into the situation.[4] Photographs enhance this prophetic calling, enabling people of faith to gain critical distance from their own perspectives on a context, and to pause and see through the eyes of others.

At the close of the book, I return to Anselm's prayerful statement of his driving desire for doing theology:

> You have created me and created me anew and have bestowed upon me whatever goods I have; but I am not yet acquainted with You. Indeed, I was made for seeing You; but not yet have I done that for which I was made.[5]

Built into the core of humanity is the desire to see God. May photographs create pathways in the journey toward a faith-fuelled understanding of the hope to which we have been called. I close with words from Paul's prayer for the Ephesians:

> I pray that the eyes of your heart may be enlightened in order that you may know the hope to which he has called you, the riches of his glorious inheritance in his holy people, and his incomparably great power for us who believe.[6]

---

[2]For a critique and complexification of this argument, see: Bård Norheim. 2022. 'Chapter 49 – The Presence of Christ in Qualitative Research', in Pete Ward and Knut Tveitereid, eds. *The Wiley Blackwell Companion to Theology and Qualitative Research*. Oxford: Wiley Blackwell, pp. 516–24.

[3]Dominic White. 2020. *How Do I Look? Theology in the Age of the Selfie*. SCM: Norwich, p. 90.

[4]Nicholas M. Healy. 2000. *Church, World and the Christian Life: Practical-prophetic Ecclesiology*. Cambridge: Cambridge University Press, p. 180.

[5]'Arousal of the mind for contemplating God'. *Proslogion*, in *Complete Philosophical and Theological Treatises of Anselm of Canterbury*. 2000. Translated by Jasper Hopkins and Herbert Richardson. Minneapolis, MN: Arthur J. Banning Press, p. 91.

[6]Ephesians 1.18-19. Holy Bible, New International Version, 2011.

References

Adams, Ian. 2016. *Wilderness Taunts: Revealing Your Light*. London: Hymns Ancient & Modern.

Adams, Ian. 2017. *Some Small Heaven: Seeking Light in Winter*. Norwich: Canterbury Press.

Adams, Ian. 2018. *Breathing Deep: Life in the Spirit of Easter*. Norwich: Canterbury Press.

Adams, Ian. 2021. 'The Empty Pool: Persistent Presence', *Anvil: Journal of Theology and Mission* 37(1), p. 8.

Aldridge, Jo. 2012. 'The Participation of Vulnerable Children in Photographic Research,' *Visual Studies* 27, pp. 48–58. http://dx.doi.org/10.1080/1472586X.2012.642957

Ammerman, Nancy. 2007. *Everyday Religion: Observing Modern Religious Lives*. Oxford: Oxford University Press.

Ammerman, Nancy and Roman Williams. 2012. 'Speaking of Methods: Eliciting Religious Narratives through Interviews, Photos, and Oral Diaries', in Luigi Berzano and Ole Riis, eds. *Annual Review of the Sociology of Religion: New Methods in Sociology of Religion*. Leiden: Brill, pp. 117–34. http://dx.doi.org/10.1163/9789047429470_007

Anselm. 2000. 'Arousal of the Mind for Contemplating God: *Proslogion*', in Jasper Hopkins and Herbert Richardson, trans., *Complete Philosophical and Theological Treatises of Anselm of Canterbury*. Minneapolis, MN: Arthur J. Banning Press, p. 90.

Arthur, Sarah. 2007. *The God-Hungry Imagination*. Nashville: Upper Room Books.

Arthur, Sheryl. 2022. 'An Elim Community Pneumatologically Engaged in Corporate Theological Reflection', in Helen Morris and Helen Cameron, eds, *Evangelicals Engaging in Practical Theology: Theology That Impacts Church and World*. London: Routledge, pp. 192–200.

Astley, Jeff. 2017. *Ordinary Theology: Looking, Listening and Learning in Theology*. London: Routledge.

Bach, Hedy. 2001. 'The Place of the Photograph in Visual Narrative Research', *Afterimage* 29(3), p. 7. https://online.ucpress.edu/afterimage/article-abstract/29/3/7/191563/The-Place-of-the-Photograph-in-Visual-Narrative?redirectedFrom=fulltext

Banks, Marcus. 2018. *Using Visual Data in Qualitative Research*, 2nd edition. London: Sage.

Banks, Marcus and David Zeitlyn. 2015. *Visual Methods in Social Research*. London: Sage.

Barthes, Roland and Lionel Duisit. 1975. 'An Introduction to the Structural Analysis of Narrative', *New Literary History* 6(2), pp. 237–72.

Bell, Philip. 2001. 'Content Analysis of Visual Images', in Theo van Leeuwen and Carey Jewitt, eds, *Handbook of Visual Analysis*. London: Sage, pp. 15–20.

Bennett, Zöe, Elaine Graham, Stephen Pattison and Heather Walton. 2018. *Invitation to Research in Research in Practical Theology*. Abingdon: Routledge, pp. 152–4.

Berg, Bruce L. 2008. 'Visual Ethnography', in Lisa M. Given, ed., *The Sage Encyclopedia of Qualitative Research Methods*. Thousand Oaks: Sage, pp. 935–8.

Binz, Stephen. 2016. *Discovering the Power of Lectio and Visio Divina*. Notre Dame: Ave Maria Press.

Cameron, Helen, et al. 2010. *Talking about God in Practice*. London: SCM.

Cartledge, Mark, Sarah Dunlop, Heather Buckingham and Sophie Bremner. 2019. *Megachurches and Social Engagement: Public Theology in Practice*. Leiden: Brill.

Chalfen, Richard. 1987. *Snapshot: Versions of Life*. Ohio: Bowling Green State Popular Press.

Chalfen, Richard. 1991. *Turning Leaves: Exploring Identity in Japanese American Photograph Albums*. Albuquerque: University of New Mexico Press.

Chalfen, Richard. 2003. 'Celebrating Life after Death: The Appearance of Snapshots in Japanese Pet Gravesites', *Visual Studies* 18(2), pp. 144–56, p. 144.

Chase, Susan E. 2005. 'Narrative Inquiry: Multiple Lenses, Approaches, Voices', in Norman Denzin and Yvonna Lincoln, eds, *The SAGE Handbook of Qualitative Research 3rd Edition*. London: Sage, pp. 651–80.

Clark, Andrew. 2012. 'Visual Ethics in a Contemporary Landscape', in Sarah Pink, ed., *Advances in Visual Methodologies*. Thousand Oaks, CA: Sage Publications, pp. 17–36.

Clark, Andrew. 2020. 'Visual Ethics beyond the Crossroads', in Luc Pauwels and Dawn Mannay, eds, *The Sage Handbook of Visual Research Methods*, 2nd edition London: Sage, pp. 682–93.

Clark, Cindy D. 1999. 'The Autodriven Interview: A Photographic Viewfinder into Children's Experience', *Visual Studies* 14, pp. 39–50.

Collier, John. 1957. 'Photography in Anthropology: A Report on Two Experiments', *American Anthropologist* 59, pp. 843–59.

Collier, John Jr. and Malcolm Collier. 1986. *Visual Anthropology: Photography as a Research Method*. Albuquerque, NM: University of New Mexico Press.

Day, Katie. 2014. *Faith on the Avenue: Religion on a City Street*. New York: Oxford University Press.

de Roest, Hendrik Pieter. 2013. '"Losing a Common Space to Connect": An Inquiry into Inside Perspectives on Church Closure Using Visual Methods', *International Journal of Practical Theology* 17(2), pp. 292–313.

de Waal, Esther. 1992. *A Seven Day Journey with Thomas Merton*. Guildford, Surrey: Eagle.

Delgado, Melvin. 2015. *Urban Youth and Photovoice: Visual Ethnography in Action*. Oxford: Oxford University Press.

Denzin, Norman K. 1997. *Interpretive Ethnography: Ethnographic Practices for the 21st Century*. Thousand Oaks, CA: Sage. http://dx.doi.org/10.4135/9781452243672

Dunlop, Sarah. 2008. 'Values and Significance: A Case Study Uncovering the Search for Meaning among Young People in Central and Eastern Europe', *Journal of Youth and Theology* 7(1), pp. 44–63. https://doi.org/10.1163/24055093-90000168

Dunlop, Sarah. 2008. *Visualising Hope: Exploring the Spirituality of Young People in Central and Eastern Europe*. Cambridge: YTC Press.

Dunlop, Sarah. 2022. 'Photo Elicitation', in M. Stausberg and S. Engler, eds, *The Routledge Handbook of Research Methods in the Study of Religion*, 2nd edition. London: Routledge, pp. 565–77.

Dunlop, Sarah. 2022. 'Visual Ethnography', in Pete Ward and Knut Tveitereid, eds, *The Wiley Blackwell Companion to Theology and Qualitative Research*. Oxford: Wiley Blackwell, pp. 415–24.

Dunlop, Sarah and Philip Richter. 2010. 'Visual Methods', in Sylvia Collins-Mayo and Pink Dandelion, eds, *Religion and Youth*. Farnham, Surrey, England: Ashgate pp. 209–16.

Dunlop, Sarah and Peter Ward. 2012. 'From Obligation to Consumption in Two and a Half Hours: A Visual Exploration of the Sacred with Young Polish Migrants', *Journal of Contemporary Religion* 27(3), pp. 433–51. https://doi.org/10.1080/13537903.2012.722037

Dunlop, Sarah and Peter Ward. 2014. 'Narrated Photography: Visual Representations of the Sacred among Young Polish Migrants in England', *Fieldwork in Religion* 9(1), pp. 30–52.

Dunlop, Sarah, Catherine Nancekievill and Pippa Ross-McCabe. 2021. 'Exploring the Reflective Practice of Anglican Laity: Finding Manna in the Desert', *Journal of Practical Theology* 14(4), pp. 309–22. https://doi.org/10.1080/1756073X.2021.1957074

Dykstra, Craig. 2008. 'Pastoral and Ecclesial Imagination', in Dorothy C. Bass and Craig Dykstra, eds, *For Life Abundant: Practical Theology, Theological Education, and Christian Ministry*. Grand Rapids: Eerdmans, pp. 41–61.

Edwards, Elizabeth. 1997. 'Beyond the Boundary: A Consideration of the Expressive in Photography and Anthropology', in M. Banks and H. Morphy, eds, *Rethinking Visual Anthropology*. London: Yale University Press, pp. 53–80.

Edwards, Elizabeth. 2005. 'Photographs and the Sound of History', *Visual Anthropology* 21 (1–2 Spring/Fall), pp. 27–46, p. 39.

Eshleman, Stephen F. Obold and Shelley E. Varner Perez. 2022. '"I Don't Do Religion": Using Nature Photographs to Engage Patients in Spiritual Reflection', *Journal of Pain and Symptom Management* 64(5), pp. e305–e309. https://doi.org/10.1016/j.jpainsymman.2021.07.034

Flory, Richard and Donald E. Miller. 2007. 'The Embodied Spirituality of the Post-Boomer Generations', in Kieran Flanagan and Peter Jupp, eds, A *Sociology of Spirituality*. Aldershot: Ashgate, pp. 201–18.

Flory, Richard and Donald E. Miller. 2008. *Finding Faith: The Spiritual Quest of the Post-Boomer Generation*. Piscataway, NJ: Rutgers.

Fujimura, Makoto. 2021. *Art and Faith: A Theology of Making*. New Haven and London: Yale University Press.

Goto, Courtney. 2016. 'Reflecting Theologically by Creating Art: Giving Form to More than We Can Say', *Reflective Practice: Formation and Supervision in Ministry* 36. http://journals.sfu.ca/rpfs/index.php/rpfs/article/view/426/413 [accessed 6 April 2020].

Green, Rachelle. 2022. 'Ethnography as Critical Pedagogy: Prisons, Pedagogy, and Theological Education', in Pete Ward and Knut Tveitereid, eds, *The Wiley Blackwell Companion to Theology and Qualitative Research*. Oxford: Wiley Blackwell, pp. 38–48.

Griffin, John Howard. 1979. *A Hidden Wholeness: The Visual World of Thomas Merton*. Boston: Houghton, Mifflin.

Guillemin, Marilys and Sarah Drew. 2010. 'Questions of Process in Participant Generated Visual Methodologies,' *Visual Studies* 25, pp. 175–88. http://doi.org/10.1080/1472586X.201Q–502676

Harper, Douglas. 1988a. 'Visual Sociology: Expanding Sociological Vision', *The American Sociologist* (Spring), pp. 54–70. https://jan.ucc.nau.edu/~pms/cj355/readings/harper.pdf

Harper, Douglas. 1998b. 'An Argument for Visual Sociology', in J. Prosser, ed., *Image-Based Research*. London: Falmer Press, p. 38.

Harper, Douglas. 2000. 'The Image in Sociology: Histories and Issues', *Journal Des Anthropologues* (80–1), pp. 143–60. https://doi.org/10.4000/jda.3182

Harper, Douglas. 2001. *Changing Works: Visions of a Lost Agriculture*. Chicago: University of Chicago Press.

Harper, Douglas. 2002. 'Talking about Pictures: A Case for Photo Elicitation', *Visual Studies* 17(1), pp. 13–26.

Harper, Douglas. 2012. *Visual Sociology*. London: Routledge.

Harris, Paul. 2000. *The Work of the Imagination*. Oxford: Wiley-Blackwell.

Healy, Nicholas M. 2000. *Church, World and the Christian Life: Practical-Prophetic Ecclesiology*. Cambridge: Cambridge University Press.

Heng, Terence. 2016. *Visual Methods in the Field: Photography for the Social Sciences*. Abingdon: Routledge.

Hingley, Liz. 2010. *Under Gods*. Stockport: Dewi Lewis Publishing.

Hingley, Liz. 2011a. 'Photographer as Researcher', *Visual Studies* 26(3), pp. 260–9.

Hingley, Liz. 2011b. 'Photographer/ Researcher: Notes from the Field of Faith', *Anthropology Matters* 13(1). https://www.anthropologymatters.com/index.php/anth_matters/article/view/223/340.

Hodge, David. 2005. 'Spiritual Lifemaps: A Client-Centered Pictorial Instrument for Spiritual Assessment, Planning, and Intervention', *Social Work* 50(1), pp. 77–87.

Holm, Gunilla. 2008. 'Photography as a Performance', *Forum, Qualitative Social Research* 9(2). https://doi.org/10.17169/fqs-9.2.394

Hopkins, Linda and Eleanor Wort. 2020. 'Photo Elicitation and Photovoice: How Visual Research Enables Empowerment, Articulation and Dis-Articulation', *Ecclesial Practices* 7, pp. 163–86. https://doi.org/10.1163/22144471-bja10017

Isenhower, Valerie K. 2012. *Meditation on Both Sides of the Camera: A Spiritual Journey in Photography*. Nashville: Upper Room Books.

Jewitt, Carey and Rumiko Oyama. 2001. 'Visual Meaning: A Social Semiotic Approach', in Theo van Leeuwen and Carey Jewitt, eds, *Handbook of Visual Analysis*. London: Sage, pp. 134–56.

Kašparová, Pavlína. 2022. 'Art as a Living Theology: Exploring Artists' Vocation', PhD Thesis for Anglia Ruskin University.

Killen, Patricia O'Connell and John de Beer. 1999. *The Art of Theological Reflection*. New York: Cross Road.

Kress, Gunther and Theo van Leeuwen. 2006. *Reading Images: The Grammar of Visual Design*, 2nd edition. London: Routledge.

Langford, Martha. 2001. *Suspended Conversations: The Afterlife of Memory in Photographic Albums*. London: McGill-Queen's University Press.

Lewis, Clive Staples. 1979. 'Blusphels and Flalanferes', in Walter Hooper, ed., *Selected Literary Essays*. Cambridge: Cambridge University Press, p. 265.

Marlow, Jon and Sarah Dunlop. 2021. 'Answers on a Postcard: Photo Elicitation in the Service of Local Ecclesial Strategy', *Ecclesial Practices* 8(2), pp. 165–84. https://doi.org/10.1163/22144471-bja10014

McGuire, Meredith. 2008. *Lived Religion: Faith and Practice in Everyday Life*. Oxford: Oxford University Press.

Mitchell, Claudia. 2011. *Doing Visual Research*. London: Sage, pp. 14–32.

Mitchell, Claudia and Susan Allnutt. 2008. 'Photographs and/as Social Documentary', in J. Gary Knowles and Ardra Cole, eds, *Handbook of the Arts in Qualitative Research*. London: Sage, pp. 251–64.

Morgan, David. 1998. *Visual Piety: A History and Theory of Popular Religious Images*. London: University of California Press.

Morgan, David and Sally Promey. 2001. *The Visual Culture of American Religions*. London: University of California Press.

Nardella, Carlo. 2012. 'Religious Symbols in Italian Advertising: Symbolic Appropriation and the Management of Consent', *Journal of Contemporary Religion* 27(2), pp. 217–40.

Nesbitt, Eleanor. 1993. 'Photographing Worship: Ethnographic Study of Children's Participation in Acts of Worship', *Visual Anthropology* 5(3/4), pp. 379–96.

Nesbitt, Eleanor. 2000. 'Researching 8 to 13-Year-Olds' Perspectives on their Experience of Religion,' in Ann Lewis and Geoff Lindsay, eds, *Researching Children's Perspectives*. Buckingham: Open University Press, pp. 135–49.

Norheim, Bård. 2022. 'Chapter 49 – The Presence of Christ in Qualitative Research', in Pete Ward and Knut Tveitereid, eds, *The Wiley Blackwell Companion to Theology and Qualitative Research*. Oxford: Wiley-Blackwell, pp. 516–24.

Nouwen, Henri. 1987. *Behold the Beauty of the Lord: Praying with Icons*. Notre Dame: Ave Maria Press.

Oestreicher, Mark. 2013. *Every Picture Tells a Story: 48 Evocative Photographs for Inspiring Reaction and Reflection*. Birmingham, Alabama: The Youth Cartel, LLC.

Oliffe, John L., Joan L. Bottorff, Mary Kelly and Michael Halpin. 2008. 'Analyzing Participant Produced Photographs from an Ethnographic Study of Fatherhood and Smoking', *Research in Nursing and Health* 31, pp. 529–39.

O'Neill, Gary and Liz Shercliff. 2018. *Straw for the Bricks: Theological Reflection in Practice*. London: SCM.

Orsi, Bob. 2005. *Between Heaven and Earth: The Religious Worlds People Make and the Scholars Who Study Them*. Princeton, NJ: Princeton University Press.

Papademas, Diana. 2009. 'IVSA Code of Research Ethics and Guidelines', *Visual Studies* 24(3), pp. 250–7.

Pearmain, Rosalind. 2007. 'Evocative Cues and Presence: Relational Consciousness within Qualitative Research', *International Journal of Children's Spirituality* 12(1), pp. 75–82.

Phoenix, Cassandra and Noreen Orr. 2017. 'Engaging Crystallization to Understand Life and Narrative: The Case of Active Aging', in Brian Schiff, ed., *Life and Narrative: The Risks and Responsibilities of Storying Experience*. Oxford: Oxford University Press, pp. 235–50. https://doi.org/10.1093/acprof:oso/9780190256654.003.0013

Pink, Sarah. 2021. *Doing Visual Ethnography*, 4th edition. London: Sage.

Pole, Christopher. 2004. *Seeing Is Believing: Approaches to Visual Research Vol: 7*. Leeds: Emerald.

Prosser, Jon and Dona Schwartz. 1998. 'Photographs within the Sociological Research Process', in J. Prosser, ed., *Image-based Research*. London: Falmer Press, pp. 131–47.

Quartier, Thomas. 2019. 'Shooting Monastic Identity: Reflections on Photography and Spiritual Transformation' in Marcin Jewdokimow and Thomas Quartier, eds, *A Visual Approach to the Study of Religious Orders*. Routledge: Abingdon, pp. 79–105.

Radford, Clare. 2020. 'Creative Arts-Based Research Methods in Practical Theology: Constructing New Theologies of Practice', *Practical Theology* 13, pp. 60–74. https://doi.org/10.1080/1756073X.2020.1727626 [accessed 6 April 2020].

Radley, Stephen, Philip Richter and Andy Lindley. 2023. *Letting Photos Speak: Visio Divina and Other Approaches to Contemplative Photography*. London: Darton, Longman and Todd.

Richter, Philip. 2006. 'Late Developer: Thomas Merton's Discovery of Photography as a Medium for His Contemplative Vision', *Spiritus: A Journal of Christian Spirituality* 6(2), pp. 195–212. https://doi.org/10.1353/scs.2006.0071

Richter, Philip. 2007. *Sunday: A Photo Essay*. Salisbury: Self-Published.

Richter, Philip. 2011. 'Different Lenses for Studying Local Churches', *Journal of Contemporary Religion* 26(2), pp. 207–23.

Richter, Philip. 2012. 'Book Review: "Visual Research Methods in the Social Sciences: Awakening Visions"', *Journal of Contemporary Religion* 27(1), pp. 176–8. https://doi.org/10.1080/13537903.2012.643174

Richter, Philip. 2015. 'From Back Stage to Front: The Role of the Vestry in Managing Clergy Self-Presentation', in Roman R. Williams, ed., *Seeing Religion: Toward a Visual Sociology of Religion*. London: Routledge, pp. 103–21.

Richter, Philip. 2017. *Spirituality in Photography: Taking Pictures with Deeper Vision*. London: Darton, Longman & Todd.

Rose, Gillian. 2016. *Visual Methodologies: An Introduction to Researching with Visual Materials*, 4th edition. London: Sage.

Samuels, Jeffery. 2004. 'Breaking the Ethnographer's Frames: Reflections on the Use of Photo Elicitation in Understanding Sri Lankan Monastic Culture', *American Behavioral Scientist* 47(12), pp. 1528–50.

Sandbye, Mette. 2014. 'Looking at the Family Photo Album: A Resumed Theoretical Discussion of Why and How', *Journal of Aesthetics and Culture* 6, pp. 1–17. https://www.academia.edu/10122037/Looking_at_the_Family_Photo_Album_A_resumed_theoretical_discussion_of_why_and_how

Savage, Sara, Sylvia Collins-Mayo and Bob Mayo. 2006. *Making Sense of Generation Y: The World View of 15- to 25-Year-Olds*. London: Church House Publishing.

Scharen, Christian and Eileen Campbell-Reed. 2016. 'Learning Pastoral Imagination: A Five-Year Report On How New Ministers Learn in Practice', *Auburn Studies*. Auburn Theological Seminary.

Schwartz, Dona. 1989. 'Visual Ethnography: Using Photography in Qualitative Research', *Qualitative Sociology* 12(2), pp. 119–54.

Smith, James K. A. 2009. *Desiring the Kingdom: Worship, Worldview and Cultural Formation*. Grand Rapids: Baker.

Sontag, Susan. 1979. *On Photography*. Harmondsworth: Penguin.

Swinton, John and Harriet Mowatt. 2016. *Practical Theology and Qualitative Research*. London: SCM.

Tinney, David and Denise McGuiness. 2020. *Available Light: Awakening Spirituality through Photography*. Pittsburgh, PA: Dorrance Publishing.

Van der Does, Patricia, et al. 1992. 'Reading Images: A study of a Dutch neighbourhood', *Visual Sociology* 7(1), pp. 4–68.

van Leeuwen, Theo and Carey Jewitt, eds. 2001. *Handbook of Visual Analysis*. London: Sage.

Vassenden, Anders, and Andersson, Mette. 2010. 'When an Image Becomes Sacred: Photo-Elicitation with Images of Holy Books', *Visual Studies* 25, pp. 149–61.

Vergara, Camilo José. 2005. *How the Other Half Worships*. New Brunswick, NJ: Rutgers University Press.

Wagner, Jon. 1978. 'Perceiving a Planned Community', in J. Wagner, ed., *Images of Information*. Beverly Hills, CA: Sage, pp. 85–100.

Wagner, Jon. 2006. 'Visible Materials, Visualised Theory and Images of Social Research', *Visual Studies* 21(1), pp. 55–69, p. 55.

Wang, Caroline C. 1999. 'Photovoice: A Participatory Action Research Strategy Applied to Women's Health', *Journal of Women's Health* 8(2), pp. 185–92.

Wang, Caroline C. and Mary Ann Burris. 1997. 'Photovoice: Concept, Methodology, and Use for Participatory Needs Assessment', *Health Education and Behaviour* 24, pp. 369–87. http://dx.doi.Org/10.1177/109019819702400309

Wang, Caroline C. and Yanique A. Redwood-Jones. 2001. 'Photovoice Ethics: Perspectives from Flint Photovoice', *Health Education and Behavior* 28(5), pp. 560–72.

Ward, Pete and Sarah Dunlop. 2011. 'Practical Theology and the Ordinary', *Practical Theology* 4(3), pp. 295–313.

Watkins, Clare. 2020. *Disclosing Church: An Ecclesiology Learned from Conversations in Practice*. Abingdon: Routledge.

White, Dominic. 2020. *How Do I Look? Theology in the Age of the Selfie*. London: SCM.

Williams, Roman. 2015. *Seeing Religion*. London: Routledge.

Williams, Roman. 2019. 'Engaging and Researching Congregations Visually: Photovoice in a Mid-Sized Church', *Ecclesial Practices* 6, pp. 5–27. https://doi.org/10.1163/22144471-00601002

Willis, Paul. 1990. *Common Culture: Symbolic Work at Play in the Everyday Cultures of the Young*. Milton Keynes: Open University Press.

Worth, Sol and John Adair. 1972. *Through Navajo Eyes: Explorations in Film Communication and Anthropology*. Bloomington: Indiana University Press.

Yong, Amos. 2007. *Theology and Down Syndrome: Reimagining Disability in Late Modernity*. Waco: Baylor University Press.

Young, Michael. 1998, *Malinowski's Kiriwina: Fieldwork Photography 1915–1918*. London: University of Chicago Press.

Zehr, Howard. 2005. *Little Book of Contemplative Photography: Seeing with Wonder, Respect and Humility*. Intercourse, PA: Good Books.

Ziller, Robert. 1990. *Photographing the Self: Methods for Observing Personal Orientations*. Newbury: Sage.

Index